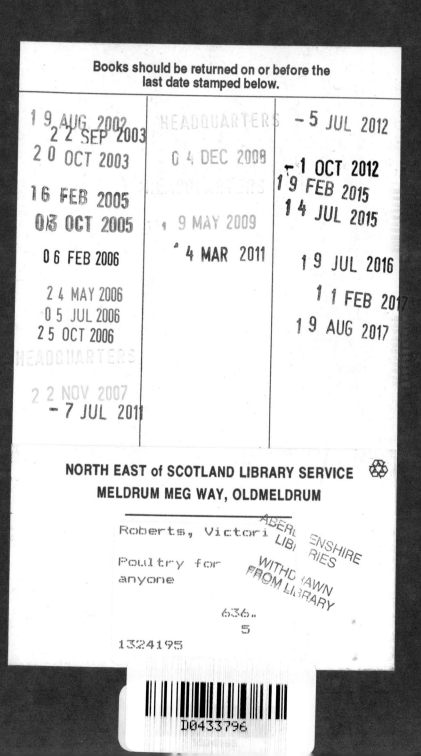

Books should be returned on or before the
last date stamped below.

1 9 AUG 2002    HEADQUARTERS    - 5 JUL 2012
2 2 SEP 2003
2 0 OCT 2003    0 4 DEC 2008    - 1 OCT 2012
                                1 9 FEB 2015
1 6 FEB 2005                    1 4 JUL 2015
0 3 OCT 2005    , 9 MAY 2009

0 6 FEB 2006    ' 4 MAR 2011    1 9 JUL 2016

2 4 MAY 2006                    1 1 FEB 2017
0 5 JUL 2006                    1 9 AUG 2017
2 5 OCT 2006

HEADQUARTERS

2 2 NOV 2007
- 7 JUL 2011

# POULTRY FOR ANYONE

# POULTRY
# FOR ANYONE

## Victoria Roberts

*Foreword by*
### Her Grace,
### The Duchess of Devonshire

*Photographs by*
### Michael Corrigan

**Whittet Books**

*FOR JACK*

OPPOSITE TITLE PAGE Pair of lemon blue Carlisle Old English Game.

First published 1998
Reprinted 2000
Text © 1998 by Victoria Roberts
Photographs © 1998 by Michael Corrigan
Whittet Books Ltd, Hill Farm, Stonham Rd, Cotton, Suffolk IP14 4RQ

636.5
1324195

Distributed in Canada and USA by Diamond Farm Book Publishers, PO Box 537,
Alexandria Bay, NY 13607
(800) 481-1353
Fax: (800) 305-5138
http://www.diamondfarm.com.

**Acknowledgments**

Michael Corrigan would like to thank the following for their help: Brian Anderton, Peter Tasker,
Harold Parnell and Tom Woolstencroft for their assistance in taking the photographs and John
Tarren for providing the pictures on pp 55, 57 and 118.

Cataloguing in Publication Data
A catalogue record for this title is available from the British Library


ISBN 1 873580 38 X


Printed in Hong Kong by Wing King Tong

# CONTENTS

**Foreword  6**

**Preface  7**

**Introduction  8**

**Breeds**:

# FOREWORD

## *by Her Grace,*
## *The Duchess of Devonshire*

I am delighted to have this opportunity of writing a few lines as a Foreword to *Poultry for Anyone*.

An up to date book describing the many breeds available has long been needed by anyone interested in 'the Fancy'. Now we can learn about their origins, appearance and characteristics and how to look after them.

Victoria Roberts writes not only as an authority with years of experience as a poultry keeper, but she adds details about each breed as only someone can who has looked after them herself. When I received the book I looked up the kinds with which I am most familiar and I understood immediately that she describes them as an expert and also with amused affection as she notes their individual ways.

I was brought up with hens and have kept them all my life. I would hate to be without them. My mother kept Rhode Island Reds and White Leghorns on a commercial scale – commercial in that the small profit made by them paid for the governess who taught my sisters and me in the schoolroom at home. Without the hens even that vague attempt at our education would probably have foundered. We inherited our mother's affection for them. My eldest sister, Nancy, kept several breeds of bantams as a child. Pam liked Light Sussex at that time and later she was responsible for importing the lively Appenzeller Spitzhaubens from Switzerland to this country. Diana fancied Anconas and Black Minorcas. The eggs were an important source of pocket money for us all.

My Rhode Island Reds were succeeded by Dorkings and Derbyshire Redcaps. Now I am delighted with free range Welsummers and White Leghorns, which cause a good deal of interest when they hurry to share the picnics of our summer visitors to the park at Chatsworth.

In the garden there are a number of Buff Cochins at large. They wander about near the potting shed. People are fascinated by them, their feather 'trousers' and their slow, stately gait. They must be the most photographed birds in these islands.

Chickens are a source of endless interest and amusement, and the reward of fresh eggs for most of the year is well worth the effort. Anyone who has the room to keep a few hens will find this book invaluable.

*John Devonshire*

*Chatsworth*

*Nov 1997*

# PREFACE

I felt, as Editor of the fifth edition of *British Poultry Standards*, published in 1997 by Blackwells, that I wanted to flesh out the sometimes rather bare bones of the *Standards*, which have of necessity to be factual and detailed. As I have kept and bred all the breeds in this book over the past 25 years and shown and judged most of them, I wanted to communicate their individual characteristics and idiosyncrasies, even eccentricities, to a wider public who may have considered keeping hens, but not necessarily appreciated the vast range and types available to suit any garden or any person. *Poultry for Anyone* covers 44 different breeds with 90 stunning colour photographs by Michael Corrigan, some of them in natural settings, with both large fowl and bantams. Technically, a true bantam does not have a large counterpart and small versions of large fowl are miniatures. The word bantam, however, is so entrenched in the poultry world that it is taken to mean either or both, and, to avoid repetition in the text, bantams follow the large fowl in every way except size unless otherwise indicated.

Any pure breed of poultry could be considered rare when compared with the millions of commercial poultry, but the epithet 'rare' as defined by The Poultry Club is somewhat artificial as it merely means that the breed does not have its own breed club, bearing little relation to actual breeding numbers or, if a foreign breed, to its status in its native country. Some of the more popular 'rare' breeds are therefore included for reasons of beauty, utility, history or genuine low numbers. I hope to pursue the other rare breeds in another volume, veterinary studies permitting.

*Poultry for Anyone* will, I hope, let you find out which hens will suit you and your family so that this rewarding and fascinating hobby will continue to be enjoyed and also help to conserve some of the old breeds.

*Victoria Roberts, 1998*

# INTRODUCTION

It takes a certain amount of imagination to believe in the fact that all chickens are descended from a pheasant, the Red Jungle Fowl (*Gallus gallus*), when such oddities as the black-skinned, five-toed, woolly-feathered Silkies and huge feather-legged Brahmas five times the size of the Jungle Fowl can be seen. Four thousand years of man's ingenuity has enabled him to develop exaggerations from the globular crest of the Poland, so large as to restrict vision, to the capacity of a modern hybrid to lay over 300 eggs a year, using a truly versatile and productive species.

Unfortunately there were few authors prior to the 1800s who considered the lowly chicken anything other than a scavenger which produced the odd egg and meal, with the notable exception of the Italian naturalist, Ulisse Aldrovandi, in 1598. Other records of poultry breeds can be seen in evocative and beautiful Dutch paintings of the 1500s. It was not until Victorian times that written records on poultry became more common, some of them suffering badly from the prevalent diseases of verbosity, claim and counterclaim, some of it centred around that most beloved of fowl, the fighting gamecock.

When the Romans came to these shores they seemed surprised to find that the few indigenous fowl were used for sport as much as food, the Romans being far keener on the inner man, but they joined in with gusto all the same. Any invaders tended to bring their fowl with them as they liked to travel with their meat fresh, and different types of fowl evolved according to local conditions. New World traders increased the genetic pool by bringing fowl back with them and improved methods of husbandry led to increased egg and meat production, flocks increasing in size on the edges of towns so that the populace could be fed easily. Then with the coming of the railways, the countryside was opened up and fast and easy access to urban markets was possible. The race was on to find the hen that laid the most eggs or produced the most meat in the shortest time, helped by the subsequent arrival of the Asiatic breeds, the like and size of which had never before been seen.

What devastated a large number of poultry keepers was the banning of cockfighting in 1849. It was a serious blow to those from many walks of life: gentry, traders, publicans, magistrates and schoolboys all took part. Some went underground, but the majority turned their energies to the new sport of exhibiting their poultry instead and thus the great shows were born. It also made room for a ruling body, so The Poultry Club sprang into existence after the first *Standards* were produced in 1865. The Poultry Club has been the guardian of the Standards ever since, with the individual breed clubs working out the fine detail. The latest edition of the *British Poultry Standards*, published in 1997 by Blackwells, contains all the details judges and breeders need to know about the points of each breed and has colour photographs for the first time. The Poultry Club is an active organisation for both utility breeds and exhibition breeds (contact this publisher for the current Poultry Club Secretary), holding a show in December each year with currently over 6,000 entries. There are many other shows held throughout the country, but sadly no longer the laying trials (where breeds were in competition to assess numbers of eggs, etc., under scientific conditions) which used to be held in the '30s.

Poultry keeping rather went through the doldrums in the '50s and '60s, but stalwart breeders kept nuclei of breeds going, fortunately, and there is now a tremendous resurgence in the hobby. Not only do specialist magazines spread the word but also for instance at last we are able with a limited edition publication to enjoy the wonderful paintings of the Dutch artist van Gink, who died in 1968. Modern books on poultry abound and it is sometimes quite difficult sorting out those written from experience and those just gathering together other writings. There is a list in this publication, by no means complete, under Appendix 5: Further Reading. In order to give some idea of what can be expected from various breeds, a list of their laying capabilities plus their practical uses is in Appendix 2, following on from the general Classification of Breeds in Appendix 1. For those who have not exhibited before, a short guide to show preparation is included in Appendix 3. With the advent of commercial feeds, it is so much easier to feed hens a balanced diet than the endless boiling up of ingredients with varyingly nasty smells that we used to have to do, and advances in veterinary medicine ensure that healthy stock is normal.

Eggs have been part and parcel of life for so long that we are in danger of forgetting that they have been used as currency for hundreds of years, whether in payment of fines, rent, or as barter; they have been used as gifts at christenings, as love tokens, as well as food, even in sport – the score 'love' in tennis is from the French word for egg *l'oeuf*. Calling someone 'a good egg' as a compliment seems to have gone out of fashion: but showing disapproval with bad eggs has gone the same way. However, the delight of having your own truly fresh eggs never palls.

All of the poultry breeds are useful, whether for eggs, meat, broody duties, feather production, exhibition, watchdogs, alarm clocks, insect eaters, weeders or providers of rich nitrogenous fertiliser. All that remains is for you to choose which breed suits you best.

*Pair of silver duckwing Carlisle Old English Game.*

# ANCONA

*Standard colours*: tipped (beetle-green with white tips)
*Bantam version*: yes (¼ size)

**History**  In 1862 the *Journal of Horticulture* said disparagingly of Anconas that 'they're very seldom seen and very little admired'. They were first imported from the province of Ancona in Italy in 1851, and it took nearly fifty years before these useful birds were appreciated, but another import in 1898 set tongues wagging and a breed club was set up. In the beginning they were compared unfavourably with the Minorca and Leghorn, both of which laid larger eggs and were larger birds, but Anconas held their own in egg production compared to food consumption. They did well in laying trials in the '30s.

**Current position**  Popular as both exhibition birds and egg layers, they are hardy birds and do well when allowed to forage, the bantams being more numerous.

**Characteristics**  The Ancona is a very smart looking bird with its beetle-green black ground colour, marked evenly all over as though a white paintbrush had been flicked at it. The white tips are at the end of each feather and should be V shaped, including the long flowing tail. It is quite difficult to get a really even marking, but the contrast of the large red single comb and wattles, white almond-shaped earlobes and black-mottled yellow legs is striking. White in the face of the bird is a major fault and the comb of the male should be straight up, while that of the female falls gracefully to one side. A rose comb is also standard in Anconas, but these are less numerous. Eyes are orange-red in colour.

**Utility aspects**  A full one pound lighter than the Leghorn, the cocks should weigh 6½lb (2.95kg), the hens having ample room for egg laying in the depth of their bodies. This is a hardy breed which likes nothing more than to forage all day and flies well. They are not so much nervous as extremely active and busy, preferring immediate flight to real or imagined danger. Being classed as a light breed, Anconas lay well and, due to their white earlobe, lay a white egg. All breeds with white earlobes can only lay a white egg as the two are genetically linked but, confusingly, you can still get a white egg from birds with red earlobes. Sometimes in shows the earlobes have a yellow tinge and this is because of maize being fed to the bird to enhance the colour of beak and legs. They do not seem to need much in the way of commercial feed, getting much of their sustenance from foraging, although a balanced diet is especially important for the minerals needed in laying. It is important to provide them with a balanced feed when either daylight is short or temperature too low for invertebrates to be about. They do not take kindly to being confined, although will calm down if trained to a show pen with tidbits. The chicks are vigorous and mature quickly, having black backs and white undersides at birth, the black feathers then spread over the body with more white tips arriving at later moults. Some birds get more and more white as they get older.

**Special requirements**  Plenty of room to range to accommodate their alert, bold and active natures.

*Ancona female.*

# ANDALUSIAN

*Standard colours*: blue (laced)
*Bantam version*: yes (¼ size)

**History** This Mediterranean breed was known in the early 1800s, but the colours then were black or white. It appears that the blue was a sport from those two colours and then birds were selected to have the black lacing around each feather. Writers of the time did not realise that the blue does not breed true, as genetics was in its infancy, and so black, splashed (dirty white with random blue or black feathers) or blue were produced from one mating and the birds pronounced crossbreds by those who had not experienced this odd combination before. Andalusians have always been very good layers of white eggs and classed as a light breed, although sharing with the Minorca the adult cocks' weight of 8lb (3.6kg), but having the more streamlined outline of the Spanish, a well known breed before 1800, with a white face. The colour of the Andalusian has maintained its popularity despite or because of the difficulty of breeding well marked birds.

**Current position** Probably more bantams than large are kept now, but both are still good layers and most attractively laced. A good one will take top honours at a show.

**Characteristics** With early handling, Andalusians get very tame, although they are naturally active and range well. When freshly moulted the hens particularly are spectacular with their black necks, blue ground colour and black lacing. The sunlight fades the blue and can turn it rusty, so exhibition birds tend to be kept in the shade. The male is also laced, but has dark neck and saddle hackles. The red comb is single and large, falling gracefully to one side in the female and upright with large spikes in the male. The almond-shaped earlobes are white and the eyes dark red with legs and beak dark slate. When breeding Andalusians, it is best to breed blue laced to blue laced. This produces 25% black, 25% splashed and 50% blue. If blue-bred black are mated to splashed, all blue are produced, which sounds like a better bet, but the lacing starts to be lost. It is a fascinating mix of genetically influenced factors but none of it is sex-linked (see Autosexing breeds). The blue-bred blacks and the splashes are used to darken or lighten respectively the blue background if necessary.

**Utility aspects** These are good layers of large white eggs, even in the bantam version. They go broody about once a season and, if left undisturbed, make good mothers. When hatching, the chicks will come out different colours which will match their adult colours whether blue, black or splashed. The lacing on the blues comes through with their first feathers, but the background blue can vary. Some strains are rather slow at feathering up. Blue-bred blacks and splashes not needed in the breeding pen make excellent layers, and there is plenty of meat on the males.

**Special requirements** Andalusians like plenty of room to range, but are fairly adaptable. An understanding of the way the colour works in the breed will avoid disappointment.

*Andalusian female.*

# APPENZELLER SPITZHAUBEN

*Standard colours*: silver spangled, gold spangled, black
*Bantam version*: no

**History**  This active and hardy breed comes originally from Switzerland in the region of Appenzellerland below the Alpstein mountains, and has adapted over the centuries to lay well on little food. Their forward-pointing crests resemble the traditional costume lace bonnets (*Spitzhauben* translates as pointed bonnet) of the ladies of Appenzellerland and captured the heart of the late Mrs Pamela Jackson in the early '60s. She was carrying on the Mitford family tradition of poultry keeping, and imported eggs which her sister, the Duchess of Devonshire, hatched in her incubator at Chatsworth, where the black-and-white chickens happily roamed the garden for many years. Mrs Jackson began exhibiting these unusual birds and distributed stock freely, culminating in her becoming President of the Appenzeller Breed Society with a thriving and enthusiastic membership.

**Current position**  Popular with those who like hens that can fend for themselves to a great extent, these still have a strong following, particularly as the gold spangleds and blacks increase the choice of colours. There is another type of Appenzeller, the Barthühner, which has recently been imported. This has a beard and rose comb with no crest and can be any recognised game fowl colour (see page 78), but somehow does not have the same appeal as the Spitzhauben.

**Characteristics**  The weights of 4lb (1.8kg) in the cock and 3lb (1.3kg) in the hen give a clue to the energy and activity of this breed; the Standard calls for a well rounded, walnut-shaped body with a full breast, carried high. They are always on the move and are keen foragers, finding their way out of all but the most secure fencing, liking to roost in trees. They are reasonably bright as hens go, and fend for themselves, but do need the constant back-up of a commercial diet, particularly when insect life is less in the cooler weather. The crest of the Appenzeller is a unique shape in poultry as it points forward and is upright, supported by a slightly raised skull. The nostrils are cavernous and there is a horseshoe ridge to the beak with a fleshy knob at the front, with the small horn comb completing an unusual facial arrangement. The black is probably the least popular of the three colours. The spangling of the silver and gold consists of a small non circular black tip to each feather, making a pleasing contrast to either the silver or gold ground colour, with the neck of the cock almost clear of markings and the neck hackles of the hen tipped with black.

**Utility aspects**  The earlobes are white, denoting the laying of a white egg and they lay well. Dark and comfortable nestboxes off the floor are vital if the hens are to lay where you can find the eggs. Although not classed as a sitter, the Appenzeller will occasionally sit if not disturbed, but otherwise is rather too flighty. The chicks are vigorous and hatch at 21 days. The silver spangled chicks are a rather grubby yellow when hatched with a small bump of down on their heads, but they quickly grow the white feathers with the black spangle at the tip. The gold are brown when hatched, but never have been such good quality as the silvers. In all the colours legs are blue and eyes dark brown.

**Special requirements**  Due to their good flying ability, Appenzellers either need to be completely at liberty, or fenced in an aviary type pen with shrubs or branches to climb on.

*Pair of silver Appenzeller Spitzhaubens.*

# ARAUCANA

*Standard colours*: lavender, blue (laced), black-red, silver duckwing, golden duckwing, blue-red, pyle, crele, spangled, cuckoo, black, white
*Bantam version*: yes (¼ size)

**History** If the Arauca Indians of South America had not fiercely resisted the Spanish and any cross-breeding with their light Mediterranean poultry, we would not now have the pleasure of this delightful breed and its uniquely coloured eggs. Nowhere else in the world have chickens been found that lay blue/green eggs and no-one has been able to explain why. Specimens of the breed, named Araucana after the tribe, trickled slowly into Europe on ships in the early 1900s, but reports had been received of this extraordinary coloured egg since the mid-sixteenth century. When crossed with other breeds, the colour of egg blends with the other breed, thus a khaki egg is produced from Araucana x Marans. The colour first imported was the black-red and it was not until the 1930s that the lavender, probably the most popular colour, was created. There is a rumpless version which, as its name suggests, genetically has no tail. This looks very strange at first. The rumpless Araucana also has unique ear-tufts of feathers growing from a fleshy pad and is available in the same colours as the tailed version. The rumpless feature is an acquired taste, but has been bred in other countries as a characteristic of other breeds for centuries.

**Current position** Araucanas are always in demand for their blue eggs whether in large or bantam; they are regularly seen at shows and their distinctive plumage colours add to their popularity. The rumpless Araucana appears occasionally as a novelty.

**Characteristics** Classed as a light breed, they are not scatty like some, but it is rare to see the large attain the standard adult cock weights of 7lb (3.2kg). The black-reds are usually the largest. They are active and a good egg laying shape with a long and deep body without being coarse. The original imports had large and floppy pea combs, but these have been bred down to the standard of small pea comb in the male and as little comb as possible in the female. A pea comb is like three small single combs side by side. The face has thick muffling (like a beard) and ear muffs, which together with a small compact crest make the breed distinctive. There are no wattles. The eyes in all colours are dark orange and the beak and nails horn coloured. The legs in all colours (except cuckoo where they are white with black spots) are olive or slate coloured.

The delicate lavender colour is much in demand; unlike the blue, this is a true-breeding colour, producing only lavenders. It should not, however, have any straw or brassy tinge; keeping birds in the shade will help prevent this. The blue has the same breeding proportions as the Andalusian and the black and the white are self colours. All the other listed colours are the same as for the game standard.

**Utility aspects** Unlike brown eggs, which lose the surface colour if the hens are pushed to lay lots of eggs, the Araucana egg is coloured blue throughout the strong shell; but they really only lay in the spring and summer months. Chicks are vigorous and mature quickly, but there are occasional birds in some strains which seem to have difficulty growing their feathers. They will go broody and make good mothers, the bantam version looking particularly neat with a string of following chicks. They do not mind being penned, although fresh grass is always welcome, so a hut like an ark which can be moved regularly is preferable.

**Special requirements** As the blue egg gene can be introduced to other breeds and is dominant (see Autosexing Breeds) care needs to be taken that any blue-egg laying bird matches the Araucana standard.

*Black-red Araucana male.*

*Lavender Araucana female.*

# ASIL

*Standard colours*: no fixed colours
*Bantam version*: yes (¼ size)

**History**  The undisputed king of all fowls, bred in India for at least 2,000 years, the Asil (pronounced 'Azeel', the same in the plural) takes its name from the Arabic meaning noble, pure. This is fighting game at its original, undefeated and aristocratic best, the strains and pedigrees being jealously guarded as a Royal fowl.  Not only were birds never sold, no prices were ever mentioned: they were priceless. A few birds were brought to England during the 1800s, but they were not very hardy and preferred the milder climate of the south-west (see Indian Game). A taller (reputedly over 24"/61cm), bonier, but less aristocratic version was more available and was imported in larger numbers as the Malay. The Victorian books wax lyrical over the Asil, but after cockfighting was outlawed in 1849, the writers had to be more careful. The breed has always had a small but totally devoted following and contributed much to the ancestry of other breeds such as Brahma and Indian Game.

**Current position**  It remains difficult to obtain pure Asil and not everyone is prepared to cope with its inborn desire to fight. Power rather than beauty appeals to some.

**Characteristics**  Fierce and powerful from head to tail, the Asil was bred to fight. Death or victory has always been the motto, so those surviving became more and more powerful, muscular, broad but agile. The stance is upright with the eye in profile being directly above the middle toenail. The flesh is hard and firm and the chest broad and flat with prominent shoulders and short wings. The body should be heart-shaped when viewed from above and the tail slopes downwards. The head is very strong with a powerful beak and small, hard, pea comb, set low with no wattles. The eye is prominent and bright and, being pearl in colour, is an obvious feature with any other eye colour being a demonstration of alien blood. The neck is short and hard, covered with wiry feathers, none on the throat. The bare skin extends down the neck and there is also red bare skin on the breastbone, wing joints and thighs. The plumage, although with no fixed colour, is hard and glossy. The most frequent colours seen are dark red and light red with grouse-coloured and red-wheaten females. The beaks are usually yellow and the square-shanked legs white or olive but again, no fixed colours.

**Utility aspects**  Although heavier than they look, with adult cocks weighing about 6lb (2.7kg), the Asil's meat is very lean, all fat being contained within the body cavity. Better meat birds are obtained by crossing with a softer breed such as Sussex or Dorking. The Asil hen lays very poorly, but is such a determined mother that every chick is reared, with or without a commercial ration. Despite their aggressiveness to other birds, Asil tame quite easily. Hens and cocks share the same stubborn refusal to accept defeat and frequently have to be separated in order to stay alive.

**Special requirements**  Space and housing to separate all birds if necessary, and dry conditions when they are growing. They do not appreciate a cold climate or strong winds.

*Spangled Asil female.*

# AUSTRALORP

*Standard colours*: black, blue (laced)
*Bantam version*: yes (¼ size)

**History**  Like most breeds of poultry, the Australorp began as another breed. A large black utility bird was bred by William Cook of Orpington (Kent) around 1886, which he made from Minorca, black Plymouth Rock, clean-legged Croad Langshan and black Cochin, all of which were, he says in his writings, of no use for breeding according to the Standard of the time but put aside only for laying or table birds. Thus the best utility characteristics were already there and the black Orpington was promoted as especially suited for residents in towns and manufacturing districts, presumably not only for its production, but also so that it would not show the dirt.

There was a keen demand from Australia for utility fowl in the 1900s and many of William Cook's original stock were exported and kept there for laying and table purposes. By the time they were imported back to Britain in 1921, the black Orpington in the UK had veered towards the exhibition side and lost most of its utility points. The importers of the Australian Orpingtons were vilified with the most scathing and dismissive comments being printed. Undaunted, the devotees amalgamated the name to Australorp and concentrated on maintaining and developing the birds' laying ability.

By 1936 the breed was near the top of the laying trials and very popular with those wanting a healthy, docile and productive hen. It was recommended that pullets weigh 6lb (2.72kg) when at point of lay in order to produce better breeders and layers. The beetle-green sheen on the black feathers was much admired but any birds with a purple sheen were not supposed to be destined for the breeding pen. Leg colour was to be uniformly black, although in older birds a lighter colour could be expected, and white soles to the feet were mandatory. There were also recommendations for breeding with only the tighter feathered specimens. One reason was neatness, more becoming to a true utility bird. In reality, it was to maintain the difference between the Australorp and the black Orpingtons, which were rapidly becoming balls of fluff on the show bench. In the Standards book of 1982, the blue colour was added in the bantam version, extending to the large fowl in the 1997 edition. The male is a darker slate blue than the female, with a darker blue edging around each feather, known as lacing.

**Current position**  The modern Australorp has still kept its levels of production, both by the devotees of the utility characteristics and the exhibitors as, unusually, the utility points are taken into consideration when the birds are judged. The judge should be handling the birds as though for production and not just profusion and colour of feathers, so the deep and broad body with good width for egg producing is important. When laying trials were still organised the birds had to have enough breed points to qualify for club awards before they began their laying stint so all along the utility and breed characteristics have gone hand in hand. This is really an ideal situation as the bird is then adaptable for backyard production, semi-commercial production, table birds and exhibiting. No wonder this good-looking all-rounder has such a strong following in both the large and miniature versions.

**Characteristics**  One very distinctive characteristic of a good Australorp, whether in the large fowl or bantam version, is the prominence of the dark eye. You should be able to notice the black and bold pupil from behind, or at any angle. The comb is single with even serra-

*Black Australorp male.*

tions, four to six being the required number, with red earlobes and medium length wattles, rounded at the bottom. In order to be productive, the body must be deep and broad, giving the impression of a good, solid worker but any tendency to coarseness to be rejected. The skin is particularly fine and white in colour, thus enhancing the table qualities. Although not prone to broodiness, the Australorp hen will go broody and is useful not only to hatch her own eggs, but for bigger ones such as goose eggs. Her character is usually docile and kind and she will adapt well to most situations. It can be beneficial to set eggs from a more nervous breed under an Australorp as she will steady them down with her placid but still protective maternal nature.

**Utility aspects**  Australorp chicks hatch as expected on the 21st day and are large and vigorous. They have white down on their undersides and black on their backs (or blue instead of black). They always have this white down to begin with and then the black or blue feathers grow through it. There should be no white feathers in the older birds. They are strong growers but need good quality feed to maximise their growth potential. The hens come into lay at about seven months, but it is no advantage to push them to maturity earlier as you just get small eggs for a longer period. The large eggs which you would expect from an Australorp, which are an attractive mid-brown in colour, will then appear from a mature bird, the maximum size being produced by hens rather than pullets. These are the ones from which to breed, thus maintaining the size of the birds, with cocks expected to reach 10lb (4.53kg).

**Special requirements**  Relatively trouble free with no special requirements, but they do, like most hens, enjoy the comfort of a place in which to dustbathe, whether it is sand, dry soil or ashes. This helps to keep external parasites down.

# AUTOSEXING BREEDS

*Standard colours*:    Light:    Legbar: gold, silver, cream
                                    Rhodebar: gold
                      Heavy:  Welbar: silver, gold
                                      Wybar: silver, gold
*Bantam version*: yes in all four ($\frac{1}{4}$ size)

**History** Investigation into the mechanics of genetics in 1929 by Professor Punnett and Mr Pease resulted in the discovery of sex-linkage with both the barring factor and colours. If a genetically gold cockerel (e.g. Rhode Island Red) is put to genetically silver hens (e.g. Light Sussex), then all the female chicks have brown (gold) down and all the male chicks have yellow (silver) down, i.e. the colour has crossed over to the other sex. (If silver males are used on gold hens it only half works: you will get all silver females, but a mixture of gold males and females which rather defeats the object.) If the barring factor is added, greater definition in chick markings is obtained, the males (double dose of barring factor) being very pale and blurred and the females (single dose) have a sharper pattern. What the subsequent developers of the Autosexing breeds were trying to do was produce a true breeding utility bird where the chicks were different colours at hatching depending on their sex. This was a tremendous achievement as it then became possible to separate the cocks and hens at birth and rear them differently and more economically. The first Autosexing breed was the Cambar, made from the Campine and the Barred Rock. Each Autosexing breed takes its name from the components i.e. Legbar is Leghorn x Barred Rock, Rhodebar is Rhode Island Red x Barred Rock, Welbar is Welsummer x Barred Rock, Wybar is Wyandotte x Barred Rock. In fact, any barred breed will produce the crucial barring factor, but the Barred Rock is mostly chosen due to its good utility qualities. The use of Marans provides a browner egg than the Barred Rock. Unfortunately, World War Two put an end to further development and in the '50s vent sexing of dayolds (developed by the Japanese to tell males from females at day old: difficult as their sex organs are not obvious) and the development of hybrid layers and broilers left this valuable experiment in few hands.

**Current position** A few Autosexing breeds are seen at shows, but their following is limited, as some people consider them, erroneously, as merely crossbreds, the argument being that they were an interesting experiment which could always be repeated as long as the pure breeds were still available. There are other standardised Autosexing breeds, the Standards being held by the Rare Poultry Society.

**Characteristics** Each Autosexing breed takes its character from the main pure breed used in its make-up, details of which will therefore be found elsewhere in this book. The colours of the adult males are striking as they have a double dose of the barring factor, but that of the adult females is often dowdy as they have only one dose, having the effect of smudging the markings. The Cream Legbar is a crested breed which lays a blue/green egg as it has some Araucana blood.

**Utility aspects** Again, the utility aspects relate to which pure breed has been used.

**Special requirements** Due to the hybrid vigour of these birds, they need little in the way of special treatment.

*Autosexing: gold welbar male.*

*Barnevelder female.*

# BARNEVELDER

*Standard colours*: black, double laced, partridge, silver
*Bantam version*: yes, but not in the silver (¼ size)

**History**  The Dutch in the town of Barneveld spent many years developing a heavy utility breed which laid brown eggs; they did not mind that the markings were not standardised (see Welsummer). The area had been the centre of one of the most important egg producing districts of the country and they wished to produce a hen that was hardy, vigorous and laid the type of egg which would sell in the UK. The breeds making up the Barnevelder were carefully chosen to this end, comprising Langshan, Brahma and Cochin crossed with the lighter native Dutch fowl. The first importation of birds into the UK was in 1921 and a club was quickly formed. The Dutch by this stage only recognised the double laced variety as standard, but the British decided to include the other colours, none of which have the same popularity. They did well in the laying trials of the '30s, but, sadly, both their laying propensity and the colour of the egg have suffered since.

**Current position**  With the concentration on feather colour, most of the utility type Barnevelders have disappeared. They are still most attractive birds with lovely dispositions and, if kept fit and not allowed to get fat and lazy, will still lay quite well, although the colour of the egg comes nowhere near the Marans or Welsummer.

**Characteristics**  With so many breeds in its make up, the Barnevelder seems to have retained the best points of them all with its alert, upright carriage and a well balanced, compact body with a broad breast. The wings are short and carried high and the tail is full and graceful. The single comb is medium in size and tops the neat, high head. Earlobes are long and red but the wattles are medium size. The eyes are orange in all colours, very prominent, with yellow legs and beak yellow with a dark point. The black has a beetle-green sheen, the partridge cock is typical black-red but the hen has red-brown feathers evenly stippled with small black peppering plus single black lacing around each feather. The silver is also peppered and single laced in the hen (compare with the clear silver laced Wyandotte). The double laced is the most numerous and most beautiful. In the hen, each body feather has a clear red-brown ground colour with a defined black glossy outer lacing and a defined black glossy inner lacing, the neck and abdomen being black and the wings laced with black. The male, unusually in chickens, is not as spectacular and has single black lacing on a red-brown ground on his breast with neck and saddle feathers more broadly laced with black, a red-brown bar showing on the wing when closed. The full tail is black with a beetle-green sheen. White feathers anywhere (except in the silver) are frowned upon.

**Utility aspects**  Whilst laying a reasonable number of eggs, the Barnevelder is inclined to be lazy, so they really need to be kept free range to keep fit. The adult cock weight is 8lb (3.6kg) and, as they are a heavy breed, it takes them nearly two years to mature. The chicks start out mostly yellow and the darker feathers come later. They are rather slow to feather up, but spare cockerels will have enough meat on them by about eight months old. The hens go broody readily and make docile, friendly and adaptable mothers.

**Special requirements**  Keep Barnevelders fit, not fat, by giving them plenty of space, but do not restrict their feed when growing as they are a heavy breed and need time to mature.

# BELGIAN BANTAMS

*Standard colours*: millefleur, porcelaine, quail, blue quail, silver quail, lavender quail, cuckoo, black mottled, black, white, lavender or Renold's blue, blue (laced) and others
*True bantam, no large version*

**History** 'Bearded from Antwerp' seems an unlikely name for a pigeon-sized hen, but that is how the original Belgian bantam, the Barbu d'Anvers, translates. Crossings with the Sabelpoot (Booted) produced the Barbu d'Uccle (Bearded Uccle) and these two were seen in Britain from late Victorian times. The third main breed is the Barbu de Watermael (Bearded Watermael) and this was brought to the UK in the '80s. There are also rarely seen rumpless versions of the d'Anvers and d'Uccle. The Dutch and Belgian peoples share a liking for bantams and have appreciated their qualities for hundreds of years, developing a wide range of colours and styles. The Belgian bantams are available in a wide range of attractive colours and have remained deservedly popular for many decades, needing little space.

*Porcelaine Barbu d'Uccle bantam female.*

26

*Millefleur Barbu d'Uccle bantam male.*

**Current position** Belgian bantams have a huge following all over the world and new colours are continuously being developed.

**Characteristics** The Barbu d'Anvers is always rose combed and clean legged. The Barbu d'Uccle is always single combed and feather legged. The Barbu de Watermael is always crested and clean legged. Confusion can be rife when, for instance, the Millefleur is referred to. Most people mean the Millefleur d'Uccle, as they are the most popular and numerous, but as the same colour exists in the d'Anvers, there is room for misunderstanding. The Barbu de Watermael is standardised only in black, blue, blue quail and quail at present. With so many colours to choose from most people can find one that they like, but the type of the bird is more important than colour when showing. The d'Anvers cock, despite weighing

27

*Quail Barbu d'Anvers bantam male.*

only 26oz (740g) has tremendous presence and is a real show-off, standing bolt upright with his head thrown back as though about to crow. They have a habit of attacking anything and everything in sight, and although this is amusing from something so small, such aggression can get positively dangerous in large breeds. They are so quick on their feet that they usually come off best when attacking large fowl, rather like David and Goliath. They have short backs with wings held sloping towards the ground and the breast carried well up. The tail is almost vertical with narrow, only slightly curved sickle feathers. The comb in the d'Anvers is rose with the leader following the line of the neck and the eyes prominent despite the profuse facial feathering which slopes backwards and covers the ears and earlobes. The beard is formed of three sections and known as trilobed. The strong arch of the neck hackle is called the *boule* and is vital to the type. The hens are delightfully plump, lively and vocal, looking like mischievous toy owls, with not quite such a pronounced *boule* as the males. Strange hens put together will probably fight, so if they can see each other through netting for a day or two first this may help. The Barbu d'Uccle is not such a feisty character, being rather more majestic and sedate with heavily feathered legs and a single comb; it is fractionally larger than the d'Anvers. The rest of the bird is similar to the d'Anvers. The Barbu de Watermael is the smallest Belgian bantam and is perky, always having a small crest plus a rose comb with three small leaders, clean legs and carries its tail lower than the other two. They all become very tame and confiding with regular handling. The d'Uccle seeming to be the longest lived, regularly attaining ten years.

The main colours seen in the Belgian bantams are the millefleur, porcelaine and black mottled (these take two years to attain their best colour) in the d'Uccle and the quail colours

*Silver Quail Barbu d'Anvers bantam female.*

*Quail Watermael bantam male.*

in the d'Anvers. The millefleur (a thousand flowers) is a most attractive mix with each feather an orange-red ground colour plus a black pea-shaped spot tipped with a white triangle, the same pattern in both sexes. The porcelaine has the same arrangement, but the ground colour is light straw instead of orange-red and blue instead of black, again with a white triangular tip. It is a subtle and delicate colour and is aptly named. The black mottled is basically black with evenly spaced white tips. The quail is so called due to its similarity to the markings of a Japanese laying quail (*Coturnix species*) with a dark back and light underparts. The cock has nankin coloured beard, breast and thighs. This colour was named after the Chinese yellowish cloth, nankeen, and there is also a rare breed bantam called Nankin, the same colour. The rest of him is umber (chocolate-black with a soft silvery lustre) and ochre. The breast of the hen is nankin, as are the shafts on the back feathers with umber ground colour. The blue quail has black replaced by blue and the silver quail is silver instead of nankin. The lavender quail is lavender on the back and straw on the underparts. The cuckoo is banded light grey and dark grey across each feather with the black a glossy beetle-green and the white pure white. The lavender is a true-breeding pale silvery blue all over

*Quail Watermael bantam female.*

and the blue is slate blue with darker lacing. Legs and feet vary in colour depending on plumage, for instance dark legs with dark colours, but any yellow in the legs is a disqualification.

**Utility aspects** The eggs from Belgian bantams are tiny and are wonderful for children who are reluctant egg eaters. The birds are good sitters and mothers, but the quantity of eggs is not great. The d'Uccle does little damage in a garden due to the feathers on its legs. The chicks hatch well in an incubator, sometimes 20½ days instead of the usual 21, but take care that drinkers and feeders are low enough for them to reach and they are kept dry when being reared. They all fly well, so fencing needs to be sound.

**Special requirements** Aviary type pens may be needed for the best fliers, or total free range, but roosting unsafely in trees may then be a problem. Keep dry when rearing and make sure all equipment and housing is of a proportionate size.

# BOOTED BANTAM

*Standard colours*: black, white, black mottled, millefleur, porcelaine
*True bantam, no large version*

**History** Any chicken that did not produce either meat or eggs in quantity was considered fit only for the ladies to toy with in their leisure, according to the books of the early 1800s. Dwarf poultry had been known for hundreds of years and both Pliny and, later, Aldrovandi mention them as being small and unproductive. Mostly known either as dwarfs or pigmies, the term bantam was a Victorian invention, supposedly because some dwarf poultry came in on a boat from the village of Bantam in Java (Dutch East Indies). Any diminutive breed was then dubbed a bantam even if it was a miniature of a large breed, like the Old English Game. Booted bantams are one of the oldest and came to the UK via The Netherlands where they are known as *Sabelpoot*. They were used in the creation of the Belgian Barbu d'Uccle.

**Current position** Although classed as rare, these are gaining in popularity again and they are an easier breed than some. (Bear in mind the somewhat artificial Poultry Club definition of a rare breed, i.e. any breed with insufficient numbers in the UK, regardless of status in its own country, to warrant its own breed club. If enough enthusiastic breeders get together to start a breed club for a rare breed, then it would no longer be classed as rare.)

**Characteristics** The Booted is a lively bird with a strutting action. The hackles are not as pronounced as in the Belgian and there is no beard or muffling. The small single comb is upright and the red earlobes and wattles are also small. Slightly larger than the Belgian, the Booted has a short and compact body with long drooping wings and stiff feathers on its hocks (compare vulture hocks being a fault in the Cochin and Pekin, see p. 40). Feathers should grow from the shank, outer and middle toes and Victorian drawings show abundant foot feather curling up at the edges. The large tail is upright and the sickles are a little longer and curved. White was the colour mentioned most often in Victorian times and this should be pure snow white with white beak and legs, plus red eyes. The black has a lovely beetle-green sheen with black beak and legs and red or dark eyes. Earlobes are red in all colours and the other colours of black mottled, millefleur and porcelaine are the same as for the Belgian bantams.

**Utility aspects** They will lay in the spring and summer and sit their own or other small eggs. It is best to separate any sitting hen from the others so that she has peace and quiet and only the eggs you want hatched under her. With only a pair, the cock can be kept within sight and sound of his hen. Sometimes the cock will help the hen brood, but this is unusual in poultry. They become very tame and confiding.

**Special requirements** Dry winter quarters and dry rearing conditions suit the feathers on the legs and feet. Make sure drinkers, feeders and housing are low enough for chicks to reach.

*Pair of black and porcelaine cock booted bantams.*

# BRAHMA

*Standard colours*: dark, light, white, gold, buff columbian
*Bantam version*: yes (¼ size)

**History** Harrison Weir devotes no less than 28 pages in his book *Our Poultry* to the controversy surrounding the arrival, development and naming of the Brahma from 1850 to 1880. It certainly kept the poultry fanciers and printers occupied in trying to unravel the progression of an Asiatic fowl from China, to America, to England; and it eventually acquired an Indian name. This was at the same time as the Cochin had appeared and taken the country by storm with its enormous size. The Brahma was supposed to be bigger still, even when first imported under the name of Chittagong, and the cocks have always been taller, although not necessarily heavier than the Cochins. Prices were maintained with a dark Brahma making 100 guineas in 1853 at Birmingham. In the same style as Cochins, Brahmas have kept their devotees although one Edwardian writer called them a rich man's fowl as they ate a lot and were merely decorative. Numbers have fluctuated over the years and inbreeding has sometimes been a problem.

**Current position** Brahmas are well represented at shows and even those who do not show them are dedicated to the breed: there is something very special about their character and colours not found in other breeds which appeals to a sense of beauty and stateliness.

**Characteristics** The Brahma is often confused with the Cochin to the inexperienced eye; it is a large bodied fowl which, due to its height, does not appear as full and broad as it actually is, one young visitor calling them 'those six-foot-tall-with-hairy-legs ones'. The back

*Dark Brahma male.*

34

*Pair of light Brahmas.*

*Gold Brahma female.*

appears short due to the required sweep from hackle to tail, without the Cochin cushion, so the tail is visible. The plumage, although profuse, is much tighter and harder than the Cochin. The head is small for such a large bird, but has characteristic beetle brows (a legacy from the Asil) which overhang the eyes giving an aristocratic look in the cock and a coquettish look in the hen, plus a neat pea comb, and in some strains a slight dip at the back of the skull. The legs are profusely feathered, down to the outer and middle toes, but preferably without vulture hocks (hard feathers on the hocks). The original colour was the light, i.e. a white body, black striped neck hackle, black in the wings and a black tail. The dark with its fine grey pencilling in the female and black and white contrast in the male was developed later. The gold, although appearing similar to the partridge Cochin, has subtle differences in the female such as the pencilling following the feather outline whereas in the Cochin it is in crescent form, the male having the usual black-red (storybook) colour. The buff Columbian is similar to the light, except a golden buff instead of white. In all colours eyes are red, comb and earlobes red and legs bright yellow.

**Utility aspects** These are stately, docile, sensible birds who make good broodies, covering a fair number of eggs with their large body size. Their own eggs are small and there are not many of them in any of the colours. The pea comb and feathered legs are evident at dayold and they take about two years to mature fully, so need good feeding to grow the frame and then fill it. Spare young cockerels make good casseroles as it does not matter then that the meat is mostly on the legs.

**Special requirements** Good feeding and dry conditions suit Brahmas best and they will generally stay behind low fencing of 2-3' (60-100cm) height.

# COCHIN

*Standard colours*: black, blue (not laced), buff, cuckoo, partridge, grouse, white
*Bantam version*: no (but in America and in old books the Pekin bantam is confusingly
   called the Cochin bantam)

**History** The furore this huge ginger bird caused when it arrived in England from China in 1845 was because no-one had seen poultry so large or such an unusual colour (apart from the little Nankin bantam) and it created a competitive spirit of exhibiting, kudos and oneupmanship that has proliferated ever since. Before the arrival of the Cochin, or Shanghai as it was first called, poultry were merely to provide eggs, meat or to fight for entertainment.

Queen Victoria received the original birds, which of course helped in their popularity and notoriety. The size of the birds was greatly exaggerated and it was said their crow was like the roar of a lion. The wealth of feather seen today is not portrayed in the books of the time on the legs, but the body feather was magnificent as it was believed that the Chinese had bred these fluffy birds for filling duvets. The Victorians later developed the heavily furnished hock, leg and foot feather that we would recognise today.

*Buff Cochin female.*

**Current position** Like the other Victorian loves of topiary and statuary, the Cochin is more a thing of beauty than utility, but it has a strong band of devotees and is always admired for its dignity, colours, shape and broodiness.

**Characteristics** There should be no sharp angles on a Cochin: it is a breed of roundness. Unfortunately the rotundity extends to its metabolism, as the birds are prone to fat and heart problems, compounded by their desire to be idle and decorative. Unless kept on short grass they will not venture far and long vegetation tends to break the feathers on the feet. They need little fencing to contain them, however. Although it is lovely to see the feather-perfect specimens in the show pens, they are not going to be the fittest as they will have been kept indoors, so when purchasing Cochins a few broken foot feathers will indicate that the bird has been outdoors and is therefore a fitter and possibly better breeder. Even in the early 1900s it was recommended that cocks under three years old were more reliable for breeding.

There is a wide variety of colours available, the most popular and original being the buff which is an even bright ginger all over, down to the skin, free from black feathers in the tail. The white needs to be kept out of the sun to prevent the yellow sappiness induced by ultraviolet light if exhibiting is considered, and is difficult to keep clean. The blue should not be laced, but an even blue all over, the cockerels of course being slightly darker on the hackle and saddle feathers in all the self (single) colours. The cuckoo is softly banded across the feathers with alternating grey and dark grey, and the black has a beautiful green sheen. The

*Cuckoo Cochin male.*

LEFT *Buff Cochin male, partridge, black and white females.*

partridge is the most spectacular of the colours as the cocks and hens are completely different. The cock is the typical storybook colouring of orange-red hackle and saddle with black stripes, black breast and tail with a green sheen, but the hen has fine crescentic pencilling of dark brown on a rich brown background. This pencilling is most attractive and on the best specimens extends from under the chin even to the foot feather. The hackle is gold with a black stripe and the grouse is a darker version of the partridge. The comb is small and neat, but the red earlobes should hang down to the low level of the wattles. The legs of all the colours should be yellow, this being less easy to obtain in the darker colours. Eyes are red in all colours except the black and blue when they are allowed to be dark.

The abiding impression of a Cochin is the soft and profuse feathering with an enormous and wide cushion that virtually obscures the tail, giving a shape when viewed from the rear of three dinner plates, one set on top of the other two. The older strains of birds tend to have a small dewlap under the chin. There should be no vulture hocks (hard feathers) on the hock of the birds and also no break between the hock feathers and the feathers on the shank, with feathering to the middle and outer toes at least. Once the Cochin is mature, the front should drop, well illustrated in the photographs.

**Utility aspects** The Cochin hens, even when young, have a matronly look and in fact make excellent broodies, being calm, maternal and able to keep large numbers of chicks warm with the profuse feathering. The feathers make a very good filling for cushions, but the number of expected eggs per year is small and the size of the eggs varies with the colours, the buff producing the smallest egg which is surprising when it tends to be the largest variety: how such a huge bird arises from what is little more than a bantam egg is a marvel. The chicks hatch reasonably strongly but can take a day longer than the usual 21 days. The feathers on their legs are visible at this stage and the quantity of adult foot feather can be estimated with the correct down all the way along the middle toe. They are docile, so if kept with aggressive breeds may be pushed off their food. Any setback will restrict their growth rate alarmingly. They need good quality feed in order to mature, which takes about two years. Once they have got past the teenage vocally complaining stage they grow steadily, but do avoid putting them on cold wet grass. The meat carrying capacity of the Cochin is similar to other breeds, but tends to be distributed mostly to the legs as the wings are small and therefore do not need much breast muscle for support. The cocks should weigh 10-13lb (4.5-5.9kg) and the hens 9-11lb (4.1-5kg).

**Special requirements** Keep Cochins off damp grass as youngsters and feed ad lib to realise their greatest growth potential. They are so docile that it is frequently possible to run adult birds of both sexes together out of the breeding season with no problems.

# CROAD LANGSHAN

*Standard colours*: black, white
*Bantam version*: yes (¼ size)

**History** When Major Croad returned from Langshan in China with some black chickens in 1872 he can hardly have realised the furore and controversy he and they would create. The Victorians were still reeling from the sight of the enormous Cochins and Brahmas and tremendous rivalry ensued as to who had the biggest and the best. Poultry books of that time contain the most vicious attacks on other breeders: probably those who were winning more prizes at the shows. The Croad Langshan, as it was dubbed, was immediately classed as a black Cochin and the devotees of the former spent the next thirty-five years proving that it was a separate and distinct breed, so much so that Miss Croad, the Major's daughter, imported more Langshans direct from China on numerous occasions to prevent any accusation of other breeds, i.e. the Cochins, being crossed with them. Unfortunately the shape of the two breeds in question was rather similar, before the Cochin's feathered legs became so exaggerated, which served to fuel the controversy, but helped to maintain the Croad Langshan's popularity through the following decades, the birds also doing well in the laying trials of the '30s. An offshoot of the Croad Langshan became the Modern Langshan with long, clean legs, a wine-glass shaped body and standardised in black, white and blue; more an exhibitor's bird, lacking the utility qualities of the Croad.

**Current position** Due to its strong utility qualities of eggs and meat, the Croad Langshan has a large and devoted following, being praised in all the modern poultry books where it is mentioned, as being an easy bird to keep, but still producing a challenge for the show bench.

**Characteristics** One of the most unusual characteristics of this docile and elegant breed is that the tail should be on the same level as the head, both in cocks and hens. This makes a graceful curve to the back, with the small and neat head carried well back. Fineness of bone in such a large bird, males being 9lb (4.1kg) minimum, increases the meat capacity and lends an aristocratic air to both cocks and hens. The dark legs have slight feathering on just the outside and only on the outer toe, with red skin showing through the feathers on the males. Odd white foot feathers are considered a characteristic of a good strain. The toenails must be white and black spots on the sole of the pink feet are a serious fault. Any confusion with the Cochin, either in Victorian times or now is quickly cleared with reference to the leg colour (yellow in Cochins). Some people consider black poultry dull compared to more extravagant colours or patterns, but the brilliant green sheen on the Croad Langshan is most impressive, any purple tinge being objected to in the Standard. In both colours the eyes should be dark brown or hazel.

**Utility aspects** The shape of the breed has been refined over the years to maintain its strong utility qualities with a good deep breast carrying a substantial amount of meat, short thighs encouraging tenderness of meat as lanky thighs are usually stringy, and a deep abdomen in the hens for the production of plenty of eggs. Brown shelled eggs were unheard of in England before the Asiatic breeds were introduced in the mid 1850s, and the Croad lays a brown egg with a tinge of plum colouring, unique in poultry. Brown eggs are considered in the UK to be healthier and more nutritious than other colours, but this is pure fallacy; the taste and nutrition come from food eaten and a fresh laid egg beats any other, whatever the colour of its shell. Breeding the black Croad Langshan is not difficult as the hens are good sitters and very attentive mothers. They can cover at least a dozen eggs as they are so large, and their docility and quietness makes even a beginner successful, whether chicken or human. When the chicks hatch after 21 days they have a large proportion of white on their undersides (unexpected in a black bird for those who have not seen it before), and they are born with down on their legs in the same place where the adult feathers will grow. As the chicks grow the white feathers are gradually replaced by black. In the white variety, the chicks start out a pale grey. They all grow quickly, are mature in a year and are relatively long lived for a large bird, ten years being not uncommon, although egg production gets minimal after about six. The bantam version is good for a small garden and still productive with both meat and eggs.

**Special requirements** Plenty of good food and a certain amount of foraging will keep these handsome birds happy.

*Black Croad Langshan female.*

# DORKING

*Standard colours*: silver grey, dark, red, cuckoo, white
*Bantam version*: yes (¼ size), but not in all colours

**History**  There is a resplendent but silent Dorking cockerel resident in the Dorking and District Museum as a fitting testament to the breed's antiquity and popularity. This champion bird was presented in a glass case in the '70s by the late Mrs Margaret Belyavin, energetic Dorking Club Secretary and staunch supporter of the breed, having taken over the running of the Club from Mr A.J. Major whose bloodlines and those of the Oatey family are found in all the strains available today. The antiquity of the breed, albeit in a different colour, is documented as far back as 30 AD when the Roman writer, Columella, praised a table bird as being square in shape with sturdy short legs, five toes and of a red colour; most of the same characteristics desirable in the modern Dorking. The Romans are credited with bringing the Dorking to this country. Due to the square and meaty body, the Dorking has always been prized for its flesh and eating qualities, including white skin and legs. In the 1860s the speed of growth was an important factor. Whether that speed has now slowed or whether we are blinded by the speed of the broiler is debatable, but flavour and texture have long been valued in the Dorking. Surrey and Sussex have traditionally been the main poultry producing areas for table birds, some being consumed locally and some being sent to London for the discerning gourmets, so the Dorking area has been established as providing first class meat for several centuries. Of the five colours, there is dissension as to which came first, but the Victorian poultry books mention all the colours. The Dorking was used as an ancestor of the Sussex, Orpington and various other breeds in Victorian times.

**Current position**  With several colours to choose from, followers of the Dorkings tend to be conservationists with an eye to history, but these large foraging birds are great characters and, once kept, seem to stay with a family, producing eggs, meat and fun on the show bench. The silver grey is the most numerous, followed by the red, dark, white and cuckoo.

**Characteristics**  Unexpectedly, in spite of the low carriage and heavy looks of the Dorking, they are very active and prefer to range widely. With the weights of the adult cocks reaching 12lb (5.4kg) it is understandable that they can suffer from bumble foot, an infection of the pad of the foot usually caused by too hasty a descent from high places. The fifth toe does not seem to serve any useful purpose and is placed just above the fourth toe, pointing upwards, like the letter 'k', but longer than the fourth toe. It is a dominant feature and is present in only four other poultry breeds as standard. Any Dorkings not possessing the distinct fifth toe should not be bred from. Bantams in silver grey have been around for many years and bantams in the other colours are beginning to make an appearance. The silver grey cock has silver hackle, saddle and outer wing which looks smart against the rest of the black body, which in all the colours should be rectangular when viewed sideways, plus a long back. The silver grey hen is a delicate shade of clear silver grey with fine darker grey pencilling and a salmon-red breast, the shaft of all the feathers showing lighter. Beware of any red on the silver grey parts as this is a serious fault. The dark is a darker version of the silver grey except that the hen has black crescent markings on her salmon breast and a dark back. The dark tends to be the largest of the colours. The red is not the black-red colour of the Welsummer or of Old English Game, but much darker, although sometimes confused with both. The cock has a glossy red hackle and dark red saddle, the rest black, and the hen has gold and black hackle then a red ground colour with black crescent markings plus a bright shaft to the feather. The white is pure white with no straw tinge, and the cuckoo follows other cuckoo marked breeds with fuzzy bands of grey and dark grey across each feather. It is confusing that the silver grey, red and dark have single combs and the dark, cuckoo and white have rose combs. So the dark is allowed either single or rose. All colours have red eyes, combs, wattles and earlobes and white legs and feet.

**Utility aspects** The laying capacity of Dorkings is reasonable but tends to be concentrated into the early months of the year. The eggs are a good size and white in colour. As with most heavy breeds of fowl, the earlier they can be hatched in the year, the more likely they are to attain their correct weight. Lack of size is something that needs monitoring constantly if the breed is to maintain its characteristics. A Dorking matures at about two years and for a stout breed they are fairly long lived: six- and seven-year-old hens are commonplace, but best fertility in the cocks tends to be up to four years. Dorkings have their five toes when they hatch, so any discrepancies can be dealt with at this stage. They are not difficult to rear but do like to range at an early age and appreciate being reared in small batches. They are not an aggressive breed and so may be elbowed off the food by more pushy chicks of other breeds. It is vital to allow them access to good quality feed all the time if they are to attain their correct size. They are hardy if ranging but can go through a weedy stage if kept in too confined an area, particularly if they have been ranging. Pullets start to lay around 26 weeks, depending on the time of year they were hatched, and continue through the summer months. Broodiness can be a problem if eggs are more important, but they make good and quiet broodies if allowed to sit in a place of their choice.

**Special requirements** High quality feed and plenty of ranging space suits the Dorking best, and they seem susceptible to dusty environments.

*Dark Dorking female.*

*Silver grey Dorking male.*

*Silver grey Dorking female.*

# DUTCH BANTAM

*Standard colours*: gold partridge (black-red), silver partridge (silver duckwing), yellow partridge (yellow duckwing), blue silver partridge (blue silver duckwing), blue yellow partridge (blue yellow duckwing), blue partridge (blue-red), red-shouldered white (pyle), cuckoo partridge (crele), cuckoo, black, white, blue (not laced), lavender
*True bantam, no large version*

**History**  Bantams in Europe were said to develop due to the custom there of landlords demanding the largest eggs as rent, the smaller eggs remaining for the use of the tenants. Partridge bantams are depicted in the old Dutch paintings in a similar style to the Dutch bantam of today, but it was not until 1906 that they were standardised in Holland. Of all breeds of poultry, the Dutch bantam best resembles the ancestor of them all, the Red Jungle Fowl, which is actually a pheasant, both in the black-red colour (gold partridge) and style. The first Dutch bantams were imported into the UK in the 1960s and a club was formed in 1982.

**Current position**  Popular both as exhibition birds and pets, the best specimens of this tiny bantam regularly get Best in Show awards over other breeds.

**Characteristics**  Jaunty and active, but not too flighty, these neat birds grace any garden. They have a short back and abundant hackle feathers, flowing into a graceful tail with well developed curved sickles and side hangers. The wings are long and carried low, giving them

*Gold partridge Dutch female.*

RIGHT *Gold partridge Dutch bantam male and a broody Dutch female.*

*Silver partridge Dutch bantam male.*

a particular outline, plus the ability to fly well. The head is small and neat with a small single comb, five serrations recommended, the end of which tends to be flyaway, i.e. not following the curve of the neck. Eyes are orange-red and earlobes are small and white. There are lots of different plumage colours, most of them with partridge in the name, taking the Dutch translation, but based on the black-red - just like the storybook orange, black and green cockerels of Old English Game, but with variations in ground colour. Legs in all colours are slate blue, except cuckoo when they are white, and any spotting or splashing in the feathers is a serious fault. As usual, type is more important than colour when exhibiting: after all, you can only decorate a house after it has been built. The lavender is a self colour, that is it breeds true, unlike the blue (see Andalusian).

**Utility aspects** Although capable of sitting their own eggs, most breeders incubate Dutch bantam eggs so that they can produce more chicks as egg production is limited to the summer months. The eggs tend to take only 20 days to hatch instead of the usual 21 days for hens because of their small size. The chicks are like bumble bees and very active. They need plenty of good quality chick crumbs, small enough for them to cope with, and they seem to do better if kept longer on chick crumbs than the usual 8 weeks for other breeds. Make sure that drinkers have very small openings otherwise the tiny chicks will drown.

**Special requirements** Dutch bantams need protection from the weather when they are growing due to their small size; they also need adequate fencing or aviary type housing as they fly well. Check that drinkers and feeders are accessible.

# FAVEROLLES

*Standard colours*: black, blue (laced), buff, cuckoo, ermine, salmon, white
*Bantam version*: yes (¼ size)

**History** What started out as a complete mongrel made up of at least half a dozen French and other breeds has become one of the aristocrats of poultry. Dorking, Brahma, Crèvecoeur, Houdan, Coucou de Rennes and possibly Cochin apparently went into the make-up of this predominantly meat breed, but the hybrid vigour ensured that eggs were catered for too, thus producing a true dual purpose breed. The first description of the Faverolles as a breed was in 1893 and that of the most famous colour, salmon, was in 1895, but the standard was not recognised in France until 1922. In what appears to be an unplanned accident, Houdans were mated with Brahmas and Dorkings to improve their meat quality and the 'owl head' was decided upon as a distinctive feature but without the Houdan's crest. Five toes were reluctantly accepted, but the plumage colour was not fixed and the birds were known either as Houdans or Faverolles, upsetting breeders as they wanted a definitive breed. Black Faverolles came to England in 1896 and there is a charming group of salmons depicted in Harrison Weir's book of 1902. Faverolles were developed in this country quite quickly as it was the meat quality and quantity that won over breeders, plus a good amount of eggs. In 1935 the British Faverolles Society was formed to promote stock, keeping the same secretary, John Milner, for 47 years until his death in 1982. Bantam Faverolles made several sporadic appearances from 1913, but were not properly established until the 1950s and those imported from Europe at this time created quite a stir.

*Salmon Faverolles male.*

*Salmon Faverolles female.*

**Current position** Popular both in large and bantam and with plenty of colours to choose from, the breed is enhanced by an active breed club which promotes utility qualities as well as exhibiting.

**Characteristics** Described by the accurate but not very complimentary adjective 'cloddy', the Faverolles is primarily a meat breed with a broad and square body. They are, however, alert and active for their shape and forage well. The wings are small, carried closely tucked and prominent in front. The tail is slightly upright and flowing, a low tail being objectionable. There is no crest, despite the Houdan ancestry, but the beard and muffling of the Houdan is retained. The single comb is medium sized and upright and the short neck increases the square impression. The sparsely feathered legs are short with the feathering covering only the outer toe, and the fifth toe points upwards, a legacy from both the Houdan and Dorking. The females are longer and deeper to allow for good egg production.

Colours are varied, the blue being laced, the black having a green sheen, the buff an even shade of lemon-buff throughout, the cuckoo with bands of grey and dark grey across each feather, the white pure white and the ermine white bodied with black neck hackle, tail and wings. The salmon is a colour unique to the Faverolles and is a complete contrast between the males and females. The males have a striking black beard with straw neck and saddle hackle, interrupted by cherry-mahogany back, shoulders and wing bow. The rest of the plumage is black. The female has a creamy white beard with breast, thighs and underfluff cream. The remainder is an even wheaten-brown, slightly darker on the neck and with dark underfluff. Unfortunately, it is recognised that there are at least four shades of the salmon in both cocks and hens: dark, medium, medium-pale and very pale. The best are considered to be the medium, but type and utility qualities are far more important than colour. German Faverolles tend to be darker and French ones go to each extreme. Eyes are orange to yellow in all colours except blue and black where they are dark. Legs and feet in these last two are dark, and white in all the other colours.

Faverolles are sensible birds being of a very quiet disposition, making good mothers.

**Utility aspects** With the cocks reaching 11lb (5kg), it can be seen that there is plenty of room for meat. Even the hens reach 9½lb (4.3kg), so the bantams are correspondingly large, but still with the same cloddy shape. Eggs are a tinted pinky colour and in good conditions the hens should lay about 180 per year. They make good and quiet broodies, but their feathers are rather soft, so if intending to exhibit at the summer agricultural shows, just put the cock bird in with the hens for a short time every few days, otherwise the backs of the hens become bare rather quickly. Keep a look out for any feather pluckers as the beard appears very tempting. The chicks are delightful, easy to handle, growing very quickly if on high quality feed, keen to forage from a very early age, but preferring temperate climates. Their sparsely feathered legs allow them to cope with damp grass better than the heavily feathered breeds such as Cochins and Brahmas, but beware of scaly leg, caused by a mite which burrows under the scales and causes intense irritation. Easily treated by dunking the legs at regular intervals in surgical spirit.

**Special requirements** High quality feed when rearing in order to maximise frame and meat, vigilance against scaly leg and plenty of space to avoid feather pecking is needed.

*Pair of ermine Faverolles.*

# FAYOUMI

*Standard colours*: silver pencilled, gold pencilled
*Bantam version*: yes, but rarely seen

**History**  The ancient lineage of this breed is in no doubt and has been known in its native Egypt for hundreds of years. The district of Fayoum has given it its name, but it was also known at one time as the Bigawi, a small village in Turkey where some stock was obtained. The Fayoumi appears to be the product of generations of scraping a living on the fringes of society, tolerated as a scavenging opportunist, but surviving with great gusto. Much scientific work has been done in Egypt on the Fayoumi as it is virtually unkillable by normal chicken diseases, selection of the fittest being obligatory for survival over the years.

**Current position**  Although not very well known, the Fayoumi has a strong band of devotees who appreciate the qualities of vigour and production on very little feed and the lively, amusing and fascinating personalities of this eccentric breed.

**Characteristics**  It surprises most people who have not kept Fayoumi before when they breed them and find the cockerels crowing at six weeks. That is not a misprint, they are the fastest maturing of any breed and the hens lay at sixteen weeks. As mentioned before they are virtually unkillable and resistant to most bacteria and viruses. They survive on the minimum of feed, foraging all day. They have quicksilver reactions and are nearly uncatchable unless guile and stealth is used. They will never be stolen as they have the unnerving and sometimes embarrassing characteristic of shrieking their heads off when handled. If regularly handled they settle down and tolerate stock tasks, but never become tame, needing quite some bribing to stand quietly in a show pen. They are small bodied with a tail which is normally high but becomes positively upright when they are excited. The eyes are large and full and dark in colour giving them a wise look. The single comb is medium in size, but care needs to be taken to avoid side sprigs (extra side growths) as this is very heritable. Earlobes are red and legs are slate blue. Of the two colours, the silver pencilled is the original and although not as neatly marked, is similar to the Campine and Brakel from Belgium who are obviously relatives. The neck and saddle hackles are silver in the male and the body is silver or gold, striped across with glossy black bars and a greeny black tail. The female also has a silver neck but the tail is darkly barred. The body is either silver or gold with coarse, imprecise beetle-green black barring, the bars appearing to form irregular rings around the body, approximately three times as wide as the ground colour, every feather ending in a silver or gold tip.

**Utility aspects**  Very fast maturing, laying in excess of 250 strong-shelled eggs per year on what appears to be very little food. They rarely go broody, so incubation is normally used to hatch the vigorous chicks which are all red-brown at hatching, whether of the gold or silver varieties. The cocks weigh 4lb (1.81kg) and as they can be sexed so early can be reared separately in semi-confinement for poussin style meat as they bother the hens at too early an age otherwise. Both cocks and hens are bossy and tend to dominate any pecking order, but they are not aggressive for the sake of it like Old English Game, for instance. Most breeders either let Fayoumis have total free range, living in trees, or they train them to housing where at least the eggs can be found. Aviary style pens are also successful as the birds fly extremely well.

*Fayoumi female.*

**Special requirements**  An appreciation of their odd personalities is needed, but they are probably the most trouble free of all breeds.

# FRIESIAN

*Standard colours*: gold pencilled, silver pencilled, chamois pencilled
*Bantam version*: yes (¼ size)

**History** A very old Dutch breed renowned for its laying capabilities and supposed to have originated from the Friesian Islands, like the famous cow. In order to escape regular flooding, the Friesian islanders lived on mounds. Archaeological excavations in these mounds have revealed that chicken bones very similar to the modern Friesian were common around 1,000 years ago. They were not imported to the UK until the 1980s and admitted to the Standards Book in 1997.

**Current position** A small and light breed but a very good layer in attractive colours ensure the continuing popularity of this breed. The chamois pencilled is the most common, probably as the colouring and pattern is found in no other breed.

**Characteristics** Although classed as a light breed and well known for its laying powers, the Friesian is not particularly flighty and takes confinement well. It is an upright, bold and active bird with broad shoulders and a moderately long back, sloping down to the high tail. The breast is carried high and forward and the wings are long, with the abdomen in the hen well developed. The chamois pencilled is a most attractive shade of yellow/buff with elongated spangles of that colour going across each body feather on the females with a yellow/buff neck and ground colour white. The male has a slightly darker yellow/buff ground colour with no spangles except under the abdomen. The main tail is white and the sickles are laced with the body colour. Legs are slate blue, earlobes white, denoting a white egg, and the medium single comb is upright. The other colours are not as unusual, with the gold pencilled having black instead of white and a darker bay ground colour and the silver pencilled black spangling with a white ground colour. Eyes are dark orange in all colours.

**Utility aspects** With the cocks weighing in at a scant 3½lb (1.6kg) there is not much scope for meat, but the hens lay extremely well, somewhere around 230 eggs per year, and because of their size do not consume as much feed as larger birds which may not lay as well. The bantam version is tiny at 21oz (600g) and does not have the same egg production. They do not often go broody, so artificial incubation is normal, or use other breeds to hatch the eggs at 21 days. The chicks are reasonably hardy as long as they are not with larger breeds which may push them off the food. It is useful to continue to feed chick crumbs longer than other breeds, say up to 12 weeks in order to keep them growing and developing at a good rate.

**Special requirements** Being clean legged they will cope with damp grass better than some, but, like all hens, they do hate strong winds. As they lay so well, make sure there is at least one nestbox per four hens and remember to provide plenty of mixed grit to replace the calcium lost through the eggshell.

*Pair of chamois pencilled Friesians.*

# FRIZZLE

*Standard colours*: self (single) colours of black, blue, buff, white, columbian as in Wyandotte, duckwing, black-red, brown-red, cuckoo, pyle, spangle as in Old English Game, red as in Rhode Island Red

*Bantam version*: yes (¼ size)

**History** People pay a lot of money to acquire hair styles similar to what comes naturally to a Frizzle. The origin of this extraordinary looking bird is reputedly in Asia and apparently there were examples found throughout Asia and reported on, probably due to their distinctive appearance, by writers in early Victorian times, but there were also examples already in Europe and documented in 1678, these having just the wings and neck hackle frizzled. Their curious appearance has kept them popular, mostly for exhibition and mostly in the bantam form.

**Current position** The large are less numerous than the bantam, but with so many colours to choose from, there is scope for all tastes, particularly as it is not only an exhibition bird, laying well.

**Characteristics** The main feature of the Frizzle is the feather construction and shape. Each feather over the entire body of the fowl curls back and upwards towards the head. Individual feathers have a ragged appearance, but narrow feathers are frowned upon. When Frizzles are bred, they will throw straight-feathered birds. These are useful in the breeding pen every second or third year as eventually if frizzled is mated to frizzled continuously, the feather becomes so weak as to break. The straight feathered types keep the feathers strong and broad which is as important in the show pen as well as at home. The bantam version seems more popular than the large, and a good one is a spectacular sight. The large are substantially built and should reach 8lb (3.6kg) in the cocks. The colours are self explanatory if the other breeds referred to are consulted in their specific chapters. All colours have a single comb, red eyes and red earlobes, but the leg colour varies, being darker in the darker colours.

**Utility aspects** Despite its strange looks, the Frizzle is a hardy fowl and grows rapidly. When the chicks are hatched they look deceptively normal, but very soon the wing feathers start to grow and they immediately turn outwards, followed by the other body feathers. Straight feathered hens, if not needed in the breeding pen, make good layers. Feathering seems slower than other fowl, but it does not appear to affect the chicks' ability to keep warm. They are not aggressive, but just get on with the business of feeding and exploring in their own way. Due to the shape of the feathers, sexing them at the normal 8-10 weeks by feather shape is not easy, as it is hard to tell the pointed cockerel feathers from the rounded hen feathers when they are growing in all directions. They are good layers and rarely sit, but when they do are competent mothers. The egg colour varies from white to tinted. They are well fleshed, being classed as a heavy breed. The continental Frizzles have a lyre shaped tail and it is desirable but not obligatory in the British version.

**Special requirements** Apart from keeping the strength of the feather through judicious breeding, the Frizzle has few special needs, but obviously withstands rain less well than other fowl.

*Lemon blue Frizzle male.*

*White Frizzle female.*

# HAMBURGH

*Standard colours*: black, gold pencilled, silver pencilled, gold spangled, silver spangled
*Bantam version*: yes (¼ size), but not in black

**History** The original birds which now make up this breed were kept in Lancashire and Yorkshire and the earliest recorded mention is in 1702. Two distinct types evolved: the Lancashire birds, known as 'Mooneys', had the round black spangling on white background, a coarse head with red earlobes and the cocks tended to be hen feathered (the hackle and tail being similar in shape to a hen). The Yorkshire Pheasant, however, had a neat head with white earlobes, crescent shaped markings and great style in the cockerels with a full flowing tail. The Mooneys were slightly larger and laid well and it appears that the earliest competitive contests were held with these, with each breeder expounding the virtues of his bird to the judge, the judge comparing that with the next and the winner going on to compete with the subsequent bird. A time-consuming exercise, but obviously of great entertainment and fierce passion. With the increase in communications over the country, especially the railway boom, the gradual crossing of the two types began, resulting in the Hamburgh as is seen now. The pencilled Hamburghs are said to have been imported from Holland and were known there as 'everyday layers'.

**Current position** The bantam version is by far the best layer and most numerous as the large has been selected mainly for the show bench and become very inbred in the process, having difficulty in maintaining fertility and vigour, but this beautiful and graceful breed has a strong following.

**Characteristics** The silver spangled is a beautiful and stylish bird with a rose comb and straight leader (spike at the back of the comb), white earlobes (therefore laying white eggs), a long flowing tail and each feather with a round black spangle on it. In the earlier shows it was accepted by all exhibitors that a certain amount of thinning of the spangles was necessary so that each one could be seen together with the silver. When this activity became classed as faking, birds were then bred to have slightly smaller spangles in order to create the same effect. The cockerels have always posed a problem in that, if they have the correct markings for showing they tend to breed badly marked pullets. This may be a disadvantage of their dual ancestry. The hackle of the cock should have dagger shaped black tips to it, as with the saddle hackle, then even spangling on the breast right up to the chin and down to the thighs, round spangles on the sickles and tail with a most pleasing effect of the spangles stepping down the top edge of the closed wing. In order to get the correct marking on the pullets, much darker cocks were used, but they could not be exhibited. This need to have two different colours of birds to create the standard is known as double mating. You may need double the number of birds to get the required result, as well as doubling up on the breeding pens. It is perfectly possible to breed Hamburghs from the correct looking cock and the correct looking hen; it is only the showbench purist, heading for the top awards, who will take the considerable trouble to double-mate (see glossary) their birds. The silver is not the only colour in the spangle, there is also the gold which has a bay background colour where it is white in the silver, but it has a black tail. The black has a beautiful green sheen, and the pencilled varieties have attractive markings with fine black bars going across the body feathers, the background colour being the same width as the bars, and clear colour

*Silver spangled Hamburgh female.*

in the hackle, the two colours being silver and gold. The eyes are preferably dark in all colours, combs red and legs lead-blue.

**Utility aspects** Classed as a light breed, the Hamburgh lays very well in the bantam version but not so well in the large. The chicks of the silver spangled and silver pencilled are a nondescript yellow with a dark back, but the gold chicks have tigerish brown and yellow stripes. They are very active and feather up fast, maturing quickly. The specified weight of 5lb (2.25kg) in the large cocks is seldom achieved. Care should be taken, particularly in the large, to cull out any that have deformities: roach back (as in the hump-backed fish) has been a problem in Hamburghs, even from Victorian times. The birds do best on free range as they are so active and need quite some training to stand quietly in a show pen. They are very good flyers, so for domestic keeping, people tend to clip the primary feathers on one wing, even if only to protect their vegetable garden from being invaded and destroyed. In older books the skin and flesh of Hamburghs is mentioned as grey which rather damns them for the table, but they carry little weight in any case.

**Special requirements** Plenty of space and high fences will keep Hamburghs happy. They will obtain much food from foraging, but still need a commercial ration to keep their nutrition balanced. If allowed, they will roost in trees, which may or may not be an advantage if foxes are around.

*Gold pencilled Hamburg female.*

*Jubilee Indian Game female.*

# INDIAN GAME

*Standard colours*: dark, jubilee, blue laced
*Bantam version*: yes (¼ size)

**History** Indian Game have been bred in Cornwall for many hundreds of years and there is a link with the similar Asil in India going back to the Phoenicians, who mined the tin in Cornwall and had much trade with India. Although Old English Game, Asil and Malay have been used in the make up of Indian Game, which incidentally the Americans call Cornish, the breed is not aggressive and has not been used for fighting, despite the fact that it looks like a Sumo wrestler. Indeed, Harrison Weir in 1902 said in his book *Our Poultry* that their pugnacity was only surpassed by their cowardice. They have maintained popularity due to their tremendous width and proportion of breast meat and have been used for crossing with other breeds for meat. In exhibition classes they are not classed as Game, although they are hard feather, therefore they do not compete with Old English Game.

**Current position** They are such characters that the Indians will always have a strong following, but they do seem to prefer the mild south-west. Crossed with Light Sussex they make a superb meat bird, quite rivalling the modern broiler in shape, but taking a lot longer to get there.

**Characteristics** Indian Game are ticklish. Since they are descended from the Asil, which in India means aristocratic, this measure of sensitivity is an indication of their superior breeding. If an Indian Game is lightly scratched, it will start to preen. The impression of a good Indian, cocks and hens alike, is of massiveness. The shortness and width of bone in the leg has been steadily developed over this century, the earlier birds were longer on the leg and more rangy, probably due to the Malay influence. Short, stout shanks are desirable in the modern bird, but this does not help with fertility as some of the best champions have their legs set so wide apart that they find mating difficult, if not impossible. To have a vigorous cock Indian with the required shanks is a real advantage, and they need to be kept active and encouraged to forage to prevent them from running to fat and becoming unfit. This also applies to the hens and they both suffer from heart and lung problems if kept in a restricted space. They are not as clumsy as they look and, once used to it, will forage with enthusiasm. Controlled feeding helps to keep their weight stable and crushed oats have always been a basic in the Indian diet. The Standard requires a commanding and coura-geous bird, combining elegance with substance. The plumage on the females contributes much to this elegance as the feathers are hard and close and most beautifully double laced. This lacing, together with type, carries over half the total points when showing: a poorly laced Indian is a disgrace. The cock bird in the dark does not have the lacing but is smart enough with his beetle-green shine on black feathers, with bay colouring throughout, including a triangle of bay showing on the closed wing. The jubilee colour has white where the dark has black, and the females are also well laced. The blue laced is most attractive with blue where the dark has black, again, the females carrying the lacing. There is usually a gap free of feathers over the breastbone which is a feature of hard-feathered breeds. They are sensible, tame and confiding birds and due to their shape have strangely immobile tails. Their shape also makes them prone to lice and mite infestations as they have difficulty preening under their tails.

**Utility aspects** Anyone with small hands has trouble picking up a large Indian: there is just so much width, weight and firm flesh to handle, the cocks attaining 8lb (3.6kg) minimum. When handled from day old, Indians become ridiculously tame. It is useful to be able to tell at dayold the shape of the adults, as culling or separation for growing on for meat can be made at this stage. The modern broiler owes much to the Indian as the Americans in the '40s and '50s, calling it the Cornish and selecting for white feathers, crossed it with their Sussex amongst others to make the fast growing meat bird now on every supermarket shelf. Egg production is abysmal, but should be enough to breed from. The best show specimens are rather exaggerated in width between the legs, making mating difficult, but those only slightly longer and narrower will be found to be generally active and fertile. The meat of any hard feathered breed tends to be lean, with the fat accumulating internally. Unless cooked with care, the resulting dish may be disappointing, but, when crossed with a breed such as Sussex or Dorking, fat is laid down under the skin to keep the meat moist and succulent. The chicks are usually vigorous when hatched and begin to eat with a prodigious appetite. Housing for Indians must be checked that the pophole is wide enough for them to get through – they dislike squeezing through small spaces, unlike most other hens, due to their broad shoulders and round sides. Perches should be low to avoid bumble foot, an infection which may be caused by heavy birds jumping down from high places. The low placed back toe is also subject to injury from high perches. Comb in all colours is of the pea variety (three small singles, the middle one being highest), eyes pearl or pale red, earlobes red and legs as rich an orange or yellow as possible. Their skin is yellow, which people in the UK find offputting, preferring white skin, but which the Americans like best. Their beetle brows, inherited from the Asil, give them a powerful look.

**Special requirements** Lots of good quality food to realise their growth potential, low perches, wide popholes and space to range with dry conditions suit the Indians. Check more often for lice and mites than in other breeds.

# JAPANESE BANTAM

*Standard colours*: black-tailed white, black-tailed buff, buff columbian, white, black, birchen grey, silver grey, dark grey, Miller's grey, black mottled, blue mottled, blue, lavender, cuckoo, red, tri-coloured, black-red, brown-red, blue-red, silver duckwing, golden duckwing

*True bantam, no large version*

**History** The first domestication of the Red Jungle Fowl is generally agreed to have taken place in the Far East about 4,000 years ago. It is certainly true that the Japanese have developed many different breeds of chickens to a most extraordinarily artistic degree. Harrison Weir in 1860 calls the Japanese bantam 'an elaborated, highly finished, perfectly proportioned creation which could only be the outcome of centuries of trained and observant natural intellect'. Edward Brown in 1929, a practical man appreciating productive birds, does not agree with him and calls it 'grotesque in the extreme ... a strange combination'. Known in Europe through Dutch paintings of the mid 1600s, the Dutch having a strong trading relationship with the Far East, these quaint bantams have spread all over the world.

**Current position** As they are happy in very small spaces, the Japanese can be kept almost anywhere successfully. They are a challenging bird to exhibit, however.

**Characteristics** Every part seems exaggerated - the single comb is very large, bold and

*Black-tailed white Japanese bantam male.*

65

upright, the tail has one third of its height above the head, the full breast is pushed forwards and the legs are so short they look non-existent. The tail, back and head form a narrow letter U, with the tail feathers in the cock allowed to touch the back of the comb, but not to be a squirrel tail, i.e. beyond the perpendicular, and the neck should curve backwards. The wattles are very long in both cocks and hens and the long wings meet under the tail. Type is everything in these diminutive birds and in a good specimen all the lines are flowing, graceful and artistic. Colour counts for only 10 points out of a possible 100 when showing, but there are many colours to choose from, the most often seen being the black-tailed white, having black in the tail, side hangers and inner webs of the wings, the rest white. The black-tailed buff is similar but buff where the previous colour is white. The buff columbian has the same but black in the centre of the neck hackles as well. The four greys vary in the amount of silver allowed and the mottleds have white spots on the appropriate ground. The blues are not laced and the lavenders are an even colour throughout. Cuckoo is sometimes seen and rarely, the red, a deep red all over. The tri-coloured is unusual in that the three colours of white, black and brown should be equally divided on each feather. Other colours are those found in Old English Game. Any or all of the above colours are also standardised in frizzle or silkie feathering (see Frizzle and Silkie), the last with normal wing and tail feathers in order to maintain the Japanese look. Legs are mostly yellow and eyes red or orange, with red earlobes.

*Black-tailed white Japanese bantam female.*

*Black-red Japanese bantam male.*

**Utility aspects** Like the Scots Dumpy, the dwarfing gene has a lethal factor, so some of the eggs do not hatch, there are problems with fertility and some of the chicks have long legs, so there is much wastage. Not easy to breed for showing as so many exaggerations have to be correct, but as the birds take up so little space they can be kept almost anywhere. Dry conditions are a must as the legs are so short, but they do appreciate access to short grass in fine weather. The hens make good mothers, the chicks hatch after 20 days and are reasonably easy to rear artificially, but fly well from about a fortnight old. Make sure feeders and drinkers are low enough for them. They are very long lived, barring accidents, and tend to get better with age for showing purposes, unlike some breeds which can only be shown in their first two years. Breeding is best done with cocks of between two and four years and hens can be much older.

**Special requirements** Dry conditions all year round are needed, but small spaces are happily adapted to. Breeding is not easy, even for those with experience.

*White Leghorn female.*

# LEGHORN

*Standard colours*: black, blue (not laced), brown, buff, cuckoo, golden duckwing, silver
  duckwing, exchequer, mottled, partridge, pyle, white
*Bantam version*: yes (¼ size)

**History**  There are not many breeds named after a hat, but a certain fruit merchant of New
York in the 1840s was in the habit of sending poultry he liked back to his wife in the country,
the birds usually being bought off merchant ships. She was reminded of the floppy brim of
the fashionable Leghorn straw hat by the drooping combs of these particular hens. The
Livorno (Leghorn) region of Italy had had its own native common poultry for hundreds of
years which were very good layers and were black (the favourite), white, brown or grey
with white earlobes and yellow legs. Some of these were taken from the port of Leghorn to
America as early as 1828 and bred with Minorcas to increase the body size. The whites
arrived in England from America in 1869 and subsequently others from Belgium and
Denmark. The buffs were created with the help of the Cochin, the height of fashion in
Victorian times, taking Harrison Weir ten pages to describe what Edward Brown says years
later in a short table, but the original colours were not consistent, even of those directly
imported. The Leghorn Club was formed in 1876 and was the first specialist poultry club in
Britain, remaining in existence ever since, and helping the breed survive a heavy influence
of an exaggerated comb. The white Leghorn in particular quickly became spread throughout the world as the foremost layer, capable of adapting to all conditions, maintaining vigour and responding to selection. So much so that it was one of the breeds used as the basis
of the modern battery hybrid layer.

**Current position**  Very numerous and popular due both to its laying capacity and exhibiting qualities, top honours frequently being taken, especially by whites.

**Characteristics**  Being classed as a light breed, the Leghorn is inclined to flightiness, but
with handling tames down very well. The show birds are very calm. The whole impression
of a good Leghorn is well balanced, the large upright single comb in the males complement-
ing the 45° angle full flowing tail. Females have a double folded comb and a whipped tail,
i.e. as though the feathers have been bound around. There is a rose comb version but it is
rarely seen. The body is wide at the shoulders, the long flat back tapering towards the tail
and the breast is round and full and carried well forward, with the wings carried tight and
well tucked up. The abdomen of the hens is deep to allow for good egg production. The
comb should not be so large as to obscure the beak at the front, the back of the comb
following the line of the head. The white earlobes are prominent and have the texture of kid
gloves. Sometimes yellowish earlobes are seen but this is mainly due to extra maize feeding; the maize is to increase the yellow or orange leg colour which is essential in all
plumage colours.
   There are many choices of colour in the Leghorn, the whites being the most popular for
exhibiting, but the top breeders have to breed many as the birds seem to be in top condition
for a very short time. The blacks have their own difficulties as black plumage and yellow
legs is a difficult combination to get right. The brown is much loved as it is the storybook
cockerel colouring of orange-red striped with black neck and saddle, black elsewhere, with
the hens a delicate brown camouflage pattern with pencilling on the back feathers and no
light coloured shafts, plus a salmon breast and golden-yellow hackle. Type can still vary due

to the Game blood introduced a hundred years ago. The exchequer colour is unique to the Leghorns and appeared as sport in a large flock of whites in Dumfries in 1904. No other breed has been used to make this colour, so the type is good. The ground colour is white with irregular black markings on each feather, giving the impression of a chequerboard. It is said they laid so well that the name had the double meaning of filling the farmer's pockets, too. Cuckoo is sometimes seen and is the normal grey and dark grey banding across each feather, but getting the legs clear yellow is difficult. The blue is not laced, but a medium even shade of blue is required. The mottled can be confused with the Ancona by the untrained eye and partridge is the same colour as the partridge Wyandotte. The duckwings and pyle are similar to those Old English Game colours and the buff shares with other buff coloured breeds the problem of getting the colour even throughout. Eyes are red in all colours.

**Utility aspects**  As already mentioned, the Leghorn is the best layer of any breed. They rarely go broody, but will sit if left undisturbed: if necessary, move everyone else out of the hen hut. The eggs are white, linked to the white earlobe and a good size. The meat is considered stringy unless from a very young bird, but the cocks reach weights of 7½lb (3.4kg). The bantams are also prolific egg layers, with a corresponding reduction in the size of egg, but they do not eat as much as the large fowl. Both large and bantam are easy to rear, feathering up very quickly. In fact, this fast feathering gene was one of the factors bred into the modern hybrid to help with sexing of dayolds, the wing feathers on the females being longer than those of the male at dayold. The birds mature quickly and lay for most of the year. The white Leghorn is genetically a dominant white and not silver, so it cannot be used in colour sex-linkage crosses.

**Special requirements**  If exhibiting, birds need to be kept in the shade to maintain depth and purity of colour. Keeping the colour in the legs is difficult when the birds are laying as it is the same pigment which goes into the yolks, so exhibition hens tend to be just on the point of lay and only shown in their first year. The white earlobe is easily damaged when birds are kept free range. Beware of frostbite on the serrations of the comb in winter. Vaseline smeared on the comb will prevent this.

*Exchequer Leghorn female.*

*Brown Leghorn female.*

# MARANS

*Standard colours*: black, dark cuckoo, golden cuckoo, silver cuckoo
*Bantam version*: yes (¼ size), not black

**History** Whatever fallacy it is about a dark brown egg that makes people think it is better, healthier or tastier than a white one has always persuaded people to keep Marans. It was Lord Greenway in 1929, attending the Paris Exhibition, who brought some eggs back with him. The breed originated in the Marandaise district of France and, according to Edward Brown, was produced by crossing Game, common fowl and Langshan together. The Croad Langshan certainly would provide some colour to the egg, but other breeds such as Coucou de Malines, Rennes, Faverolles, Barred Rock, Brakel and Gatinaise were apparently used as well. This mix of breeds left the legacy of a cuckoo coloured bird with feathered legs, but laying a dark brown egg. The British immediately wanted to breed out the feathered legs and eventually the cuckoo colours were standardised. The French, as usual, also appreciated the birds for their table qualities, thus creating a dual purpose bird. A commercial firm has recently created a hybrid, the Speckledy hen, based on the Maran, to provide many more speckled brown eggs.

**Current position** Never out of favour due to the dark brown eggs, Marans are a useful breed. The bantam version lays better than the large, some being kept only for the production of eggs for exhibition.

**Characteristics** The Standard says that Marans are active, compact and graceful. The first needs working on as Marans can get lazy and fat very easily and are therefore best on free range. The body is of medium length with good width and depth for meat production, being judged on this as well as just looks. The front is broad and the breast long and well fleshed. The high tail complements the neat head with a medium single comb and prominent eye. Most Marans are cuckoo patterned, as evenly as possible, with each feather having grey and dark grey bands across it. There are shades of this, with the dark cuckoo being the most numerous and darker with no white feathers and the silver cuckoo paler and having quite a lot of white in it. The males tend to be a lighter colour than the females in any case. The golden is still cuckoo patterned but with a wash of gold throughout. They are not as popular. The black has been developed and is black with a beetle-green sheen. In all colours the eyes are orangey-red, the earlobes red and the legs white.

**Utility aspects** With the cocks attaining 8lb (3.6kg) there is plenty of meat to be had and they mature quite quickly for a heavy breed, getting to 6-7lb (2.7-3.2kg) at about six months old. The hens are very individual as to whether the eggs are speckled or not. Those wanting speckled eggs should only breed from speckled eggs, but in any case, only the best brown eggs should be used for breeding purposes. If the birds are pushed to produce more eggs, the colour starts to go. It is only a surface pigment on the shell and at the end of lay can be paler than at the start, so records are especially useful for breeding. At most poultry shows there are various classes for eggs and often a specific Marans class, the eggs being shown either singly, in threes or in sixes, the latter being very hard to manage as they must all be matching as well as perfectly fresh. The hens go broody and make quite good mothers, but most people want the eggs, so break them from being broody by confinement in a smallish wire-floored pen with food and water for a fortnight without being let out. Pushing them off the nest will not work, but changing the environment does. The breed is genetically barred

*Marans female.*

(see Autosexing breeds) so at dayold the males have a white spot on top of the head, the females much darker. It is about 80% accurate as a method of sexing, the colour difference between males and females becoming more marked as they get older in the cuckoo, so the males can be separated for meat production if wanted. The chicks are strong and grow quickly but need good quality feed to reach their potential.

**Special requirements** Beware of over-eating and laziness in older birds and only breed from the best brown eggs.

# MINORCA

*Standard colours*: black, white, blue (not laced)
*Bantam version*: yes (¼ size), single comb only

**History**  In Victorian times anyone trading from the Near East was called a Turkey merchant and anyone trading from the Mediterranean was known as a Spanish merchant; any poultry they brought back with them were termed likewise. The Minorca is just one of several Spanish breeds established in the UK, but we do not yet have the one going under the delightful name of Prat. Minorcas actually on the island of Menorca have had a varied past but those and some from the mainland were first brought to England in 1830, although one writer reckons they were in Devon in 1780 when many Spanish and French prisoners of war became naturalised Englishmen and brought their fowl with them. The Minorca, also

*Minorca male.*

known as the Red Faced Spanish to distinguish it from the White Faced Spanish (a rare breed still kept today) remained as a stalwart of the West Country, perhaps liking the climate, until about 1870 and classes for them at the Crystal Palace Show were provided in 1883. The black plumage was an asset in industrial areas, but, as so often happened, exaggerated points, in this case the comb, took over from usefulness at one stage. The breed has always had first place with weight and size of egg, its cousin the Leghorn beating it on numbers, but Minorcas did well in the laying trials of the '30s, regularly being in the top pens. The rose comb Minorca was developed in the early 1900s as a utility strain in the UK, some having been developed in America about fifteen years before this, ostensibly to avoid problems with frostbite on the large single comb, the pain of which would stop a bird breeding or laying immediately. A world famous cock Minorca, known as The McNab, in 1924 won the championship at the Crystal Palace out of 6,500 entries. He was as close to perfection as anyone had ever seen.

**Current position** Not particularly popular as a backyard bird as the colours are not as exciting as some, but liked by those who appreciate a large white egg and a challenge on the show bench, plus the attraction of the bantams. The white is rarely seen.

**Characteristics** Not always a hardy bird and slow to feather, but docile and sensible, the Minorca is graceful. The broad shouldered body is square and compact with a full and rounded breast and long back sloping down to the full and flowing tail. It is the headgear of the cock that arrests attention with a huge, five spiked single comb set on a large head and perfectly upright and straight. The rose comb version is now rarely seen. The wattles are long and the white earlobes are almond shaped and should not exceed 2¾in deep by 1½in wide (6.88cm by 3.75cm). The earlobe in the female is 1¾in deep and 1¼in wide (4.4cm by 3.3cm) and the comb falls gracefully to one side but not being so large as to obstruct her vision and she has a deep abdomen to allow for good egg production. There is no restriction on size of earlobe in the bantam, but any white in the face of large or bantam is a serious defect. The black is glossy black and the white is pure glossy white. The blues, both in large and bantam, were perfected by Herbert Whitley of Paignton who was obsessed by blue birds, winning prizes in 1933, and are a soft medium blue, free from lacing. Eyes and legs in the black and blue are dark, with red eyes and white legs in the white. The legs are short in comparison to the Leghorn.

**Utility aspects** With the cocks weighing in at 8lb (3.6kg) this is the heaviest of the light breeds, maturing quickly but sometimes with rather slow feather growth. Bearing confine-ment well, but still liking the addition of greenstuffs, they are economical to keep. Some strains have the reputation of not being hardy and it is generally agreed that as a breed, dampness is a killer. Keeping young birds indoors naturally increases the size of the comb and can make it soft and liable to fall over, which is a serious defect in the males. It is a one season show bird as the earlobes get damaged very easily. Minorcas lay the largest white eggs of any breed and about 200 per year is to be expected. They rarely go broody, but will sit if left undisturbed.

**Special requirements** Not needing much space, Minorcas appreciate dry conditions more than other poultry. If confined, they like to have branches or perches to fly up to for the exercise, plus greenstuffs.

# MODERN GAME

*Standard colours*: birchen, black-red, brown-red, golden duckwing, silver duckwing, pyle,
    wheaten, black, blue (not laced), white, blue-red, silver blue, lemon blue
*Bantam version*: yes (¼ size)

**History**  The old poultry books are almost without exception derogatory about the development of the Modern Game when there was such a noble bird as the Old English Game
gracing the farmyards and gardens of England. It was the outlawing of cockfighting in 1849
that led to an exhibition bird being developed, but Harrison Weir still could not understand
why all the defects of the Old English Game were then exaggerated and considered beauty
in the Modern, such as stilty long legs, small narrow tail, an upright stance and a snaky
head. Of course some of those breeding Modern Game for exhibition in the late Victorian
times had never been to or participated in a cockfight and did not appreciate the advantages
of the shorter and more powerful Game. Instead they believed that elegance was obtained
by the tall, bold, springy and hard type of the Modern. The introduction of Malay blood to
increase the height of the Modern Game has meant that the legs are very long. The fierce
Malay expression was bred out and a snaky, long thin head advocated. It was such a novelty
in the 1880s that cocks changed hands for £100, a great deal of money in those days.

**Current position**  Being an entirely exhibition breed, the bantam Modern has retained its
devotees and classes are still large at even quite small shows, but there are few large fowl
seen. Discussions around showpens can go on for hours concerning the relative merits or
otherwise of entries.

**Characteristics**  Both cocks and hens should look as though they are reaching to their full
height and training is given in the showpen with tidbits to encourage this reach. There are
only a few more points awarded for style and type than colour but colours in the Modern
Game are fewer than in the Old English. The black-red is always popular as it is the storybook cockerel colour of orange hackle and crimson saddle with black breast, tails and thighs,
while the hen is a pretty shade of gold on the neck, salmon breast and a delicate shade of ash
on the thighs with body colour a light partridge brown, finely pencilled, and the tail black.
The blue-red has blue where the black-red has black and it is a pretty combination. The pyle
is a very smart colour, an unusual mixture of reds and white with the colour in the hen being
more subtly arranged. The brown-red is almost a misnomer as the only colours allowed in it
are lemon and black in both cocks and hens, in nearly the same distribution as the black-red.
The lemon blue has blue where the brown-red has black which is most attractive and they
both have gypsy (dark) faces. The duckwings, the birchen and the wheaten are similar to
Old English Game.

   Apparently the long legs led to a delicacy of constitution with knock knees (or cow
hocks) and bent breastbones – both deformities to be avoided. The Moderns get tame and
steady quite quickly but do not take kindly to being confined for any length of time. Training for the showpen would then be done at intervals of a few days with the birds running out
in between. The Malay influence also gave the Modern the small, narrow tail, held slightly
above the line of the back and well whipped (the feathers being closely held together as
though bound (whipped) with thread). The shoulders should be broad and well forward, the
body short, the back flat and tapering to the tail. The feathers should be very short and hard,
the cock's hackle feathers being particularly favoured by dry fly fishermen. The colour of

*Birchen Modern Game male.*

eyes, faces and legs vary with feather colour, but earlobes are red or dark throughout and shanks should be rounded with the back toe standing out well behind.

Utility aspects  Of course the hens lay, but not very well, and in the *Feathered World Yearbook of 1935*, they were being highly praised for the quality of meat, which presumably refers to the large, as the bantam version only weighs in at 20oz (570g).

**Special requirements**  Certainly in the bantams, care must be taken with the long and potentially delicate legs, but they do like to range freely.

# OLD ENGLISH GAME - OXFORD and CARLISLE

*Standard colours*: over 30, the best known being black-red, grey, duckwing, pyle, brown-red, ginger, crele, wheaten, spangle, furness (furnace), brassy back, honey dun, blue dun, custard pyle, hennie, muff, tassel
*Bantam version*: yes (¼ size)

**History** When the Romans first came to these shores they found certain domestication of poultry, but the main use was for entertainment or sport, not so much for meat. The practice of cockfighting is a very ancient one, documented all over the world for the past 2,000 years. For something so ingrained in daily life, it must have been a real blow when cock-fighting was outlawed in the UK in 1849. Everyone was involved, from royalty down to schoolboys who used to pay the schoolmaster a fee on Shrove Tuesday, in order that they could bring their gamecocks to school and fight them for the day; it certainly enhanced the meagre salary. The fines imposed on the banning of cockfighting were sufficient to deter most, but some never stopped, surreptitiously continuing the so-called sport. At about the same time, exhibiting was in its infancy, so what better than to direct all the cockfighting energy into showing - competition of a less terminal nature, albeit less exciting. Many of the characteristics, language and traditions of the cockfighters were carried into exhibiting, such as the dubbing of the comb. This was vital when fighting as the small single comb was used by the cocks to hold onto their adversary, inflicting severe damage with the wings and spurs. The practice of cutting off the comb close to the head when the bird was about six months old removed this advantage and prevented much bloodshed. The wattles were also removed for the same reason. When the birds were used for fighting in early Victorian times they obviously had to be in first class condition. Selection was by survival of the fittest over many generations with some studs, such as Lord Derby's, having pedigrees going back a hundred years and an hereditary guardian, such was the esteem in which the birds were held. This meant that the breed was naturally fit and hardy with strong muscles and close, hard feathering. The method of feeding the birds was a well guarded family secret and led to much rivalry, none of it friendly. Unfortunately, there is still a lot of thievery where Game is concerned and some yards have to resort to all the modern alarms and detectors to protect their stock.

The exhibiting fervour is well illustrated by a quote from the 1934 Birmingham Show report: 'The Pyle, White, Spangle or Crele classes again contained some really hot stuff, especially so in Pyles, these being so shapely, keen and well balanced in hand.'

In the 1930s the Old English Game Club split into two with the original Game called Oxfords and the newer exhibition type called Carlisle. The Standards book of 1952 says that the bantams had been 'recently created'. It is doubtful if they were bred down from the large Game, probably developed from the common crossbred bantam of the countryside, but Game bantams were mentioned in publications of the mid 1800s.

**Current position** People, nearly all men, who keep Game seem to be a race apart with their own language and customs. Some strains can be traced back centuries. The American Pit Game, fighting still being legal in some parts of the USA, has been imported and crossed with the OEG which offends the purists. Hugely popular still, but difficulties with birds being stolen.

*Pair of ginger-breasted ginger-red Oxford Old English Game.*

**Characteristics** The original type of Game (Oxford) is a well balanced, close heeled, athletic fighting fowl with the back at 45° to the ground. The Carlisle is larger breasted, horizontally backed and a bit more staid. The main attribute of Game is its courage. This unfortunately means that they all want to be boss, so endless fighting occurs in pens between cocks, hens or chicks. Unless some decide to be subordinate, they will fight to the death and have to be kept separately. Once the pecking order has been established the top dog will usually keep order among the lower ranks. In some old pictures of Game it can be seen that the tail feathers have been trimmed, also those of the primaries and saddle hackles. This was, like the dubbing, to give less hold for the adversary, but in the showpen all the feathers should be perfect and in place for the birds to win. They take top honours on a very regular basis. They do say that a good Game bird cannot be a bad colour, but this applies less to the bantams. Over thirty colours are found in the OEG, some of them being regional variations. Lord Derby's stud for instance were black-reds, but they all had white beaks and legs, thus distinguishing them from other black-reds. The various colours have their own combinations such as smock-breasted, custard pyle, yellow legs; ginger-breasted, ginger red, milk-and-water legs; spotted-breasted, beasy yellow, carp legs. There is also some confusion in local names as the Furness originated from a parish of that name in Lancashire, but is also written as Furnace and becomes a colour. Most of the colours are dark as the melanin pigment lends strength to the feathers, hence migratory birds such as snow geese have dark wing tips. Fishermen particularly like Game feathers as they are very stiff and when wound round the shank of a hook will make the artificial fly stand on the surface of

*Splashed Carlisle Old English Game male.*

*Silver duckwing Carlisle Old English Game male.*

the water, just like a natural fly. One of the dry fly patterns is called the Iron Blue Dun and is made from the cape of the Blue Dun Game. Not only are there many colours, but various types such as Henny: cocks having hen-shaped feathers; Muffs (bearded) and Tasselled: long feathers behind the comb (lark tops).

Handling of the OEG is vital to their type, with the Oxford judge holding the bird facing away from him to assess the correct balance. Handling consists of symmetry, cleverness, hardness of flesh and feathers, condition and constitution.

*Pair of crele Old English Game Bantams*

*Brown-breasted brown-red Oxford Old English Game female.*

*Black-red Carlisle Old English Game male.*

**Utility aspects**  The inherent hardiness of the Game and its natural fitness has meant that the meat quality has always been superb. Some sought to increase the quantity by crossing with the larger breeds such as Sussex or Dorking. Game lay well and the hens are exceedingly good mothers, protecting their progeny against all comers, but careful with the chicks at the same time. They will cheerfully kill another hen who wanders too near, whether of Game or another breed. The chicks begin their pugnacious attributes at a very early age and really should not be reared with other breeds as they may kill them. The Oxfords are lighter in weight than the Carlisles, as befits an athlete, but in neither variety is it recommended that males are over 6lb (2.7kg). With so many types and colours, it seems to be agreed that the strength of Game comes through the female line, so no matter how good a cock bird, if he is not mated to equal or better hens, the progeny will be inferior.

**Special requirements**  Extra housing is needed in case birds have to be separated if they decide they can no longer live with their former fellows. Good quality food and extra tidbits are essential to maintain the handling of these aristocratic birds.

*Wheaten Old English Game bantam female.*

# OLD ENGLISH PHEASANT FOWL

*Standard colours*: gold, silver
*Bantam version*: yes (¼ size), but rarely seen

**History** The Yorkshire Pheasant or Copper Moss, christened Old English Pheasant Fowl in 1914, was one of the breeds developed to survive northern winters with a rose comb, prolificacy and hardiness. The Hamburg and Derbyshire Redcap are related, with this type of northern fowl being mentioned in 1702 which says much for its usefulness and popularity. Photographs of 1930s birds are remarkably similar to those of today.

**Current position** At shows, the Old English Pheasant Fowl is exhibited in rare breed classes and not many are seen. Those who keep them for their usefulness are devotees, particularly as the birds are handsome and elegant as well.

**Characteristics** The female gives rise to the name because her ground colour is a bright bay with black crescent spangling, very much like the breast of a cock game pheasant (*Phasianus colchicus colchicus*). These birds always seem to shine, the beetle-green black markings helping in this respect. The cocks seem darker with black lacing on the breast and a mahogany back, but the ground colour is as bright as the hens'. The tail is flowing, black with a green sheen and the legs are slate blue. There is similarity to the Gold Spangled Hamburg in the colour, but the markings are different in shape. The Pheasant Fowl has white earlobes and a medium sized flat topped rose comb with the leader (the spike at the back) gracefully following the curve of the neck downwards, unlike the Hamburg. The body of the hen is long and deep as befits her utility qualities, with the tail set well back. The carriage is alert and active as these are prime foragers. Although good fliers, they are not nervous by nature. The Silver Old English Pheasant Fowl is rarely seen and tends to be confused with a Silver Spangled Hamburg.

**Utility aspects** They are well known in their native counties of Yorkshire and Lancashire for egg production, all the old books mentioning a continuous supply once they got started, carrying on for several years. The egg is large and usually white to cream in colour. They will occasionally go broody and are sensible when they go down. Although the Pheasant Fowl shares similarities with the Hamburgs and the Redcaps, the chicks are a different colour at hatching from those other breeds. The chicks are vigorous and grow strongly, although they take longer to mature than would be expected for a light breed, the hens laying at around seven to eight months. They carry a good amount of breast meat and suit the title of dual purpose, with the cocks' desired weight at 6-7lb (2.7-3.2kg).

**Special requirements** Pheasant Fowl need to be able to range and forage as well as be provided with a balanced commercial ration which will ensure good production for several years.

*Old English Pheasant Fowl male.*

# ORPINGTON

*Standard colours*: black (single or rose comb), blue (laced), buff, white
*Bantam version*: yes (¼ size), but not with a rose comb

**History** William Cook of Orpington in Kent had a long career as a creator of breeds, purveyor of poultry requisites and promoter and advertiser of all poultry-related topics of interest. His efforts with the black Orpington in 1886 (forerunner of the Australorp) were then superseded by another breeder who turned a perfectly good utility fowl into an excessively large, feathery, apparently legless, solely exhibition bird. Even in 1925, while praising the now beetle-green ball of fluff for its appearance, the writers bemoaned the fact that excess feather equalled lack of eggs. The new breeder stated he had created his black Orpingtons by another route of breeding, so, to counteract this usurping of Cook's position, Cook produced the buff Orpington. It was not at first called this, at least not officially, as there appeared to be the same breed which had been bred in Lincolnshire for 25 years, the Lincolnshire buff, except this had five toes and turned out to be nearer to the original Shanghai (Cochin) with feathered legs, although mostly white shanks. The Poultry Club, much to the other breeders' disgust, accepted the name of buff Orpington for Cook's creation. He stated that he had used Cochin, dark Dorking and gold Hamburg, which must have taken some time to perfect as there are many factors in that mixture needing to be bred out, such as white earlobes, yellow legs and any colour other than buff. In the '30s, there existed not only two types of Orpington, but two clubs, the second one calling itself the Old Type Orpington Club and concentrating more on the meat and eggs aspects. The white Orpingtons followed on from the other colours and for a while there was a jubilee Orpington, created for Queen Victoria's celebration, being mahogany, white and black, the nearest to red, white and blue that could be produced. Although this colour is not standardised, it is similar to the speckled Sussex and is occasionally seen on the showbench. The buff is distinguished by being kept by HM Elizabeth the Queen Mother, continuing the tradition of royalty keeping poultry.

**Current position** Most Orpingtons are exhibition birds but there are still some pockets of more useful ones and they are all extremely popular, especially the buff.

**Characteristics** Despite all the fluff, the Orpington is an active but docile bird with a deep, broad, cobby body with the back appearing short as the hackle and tail meet in a graceful U shape. This shape is repeated in the underline and the cushion on the hen rises to meet the high tail. Blues and blacks are the largest colours, minimum 10lb (4.55kg) in the cocks; their legs are hidden by fluff. The buffs and whites are slightly lighter weight so more of their legs is seen. The head is neat with a small single comb (rose comb allowed in the large blacks), and red earlobes. The dark colours have dark eyes and legs and the paler colours have red eyes and white legs, but they all must have white toenails. The blues are attractively laced but the buff is probably the most difficult colour as it should be even throughout and down to the skin with no white or dark feathers. The odd cinnamon tail feather in the buff is proof of sound colour and infinitely preferable to a white one. The buff colour fades particularly easily in sunshine, so show specimens tend to be kept in the shade. They do not mind being confined some of the time, but will lose condition if kept indoors too long. Some of the colours tend to be not as close feathered as the Standard calls for, heading more towards Cochin type of soft and loose feathering. This can lead to problems

*Buff Orpington male.*

in the breeding pen where the feet of the cocks scrape away the back feathers from their favourite hens and can damage the skin. Youngsters can be prone to be feather-pecked, too, particularly in high temperatures. Larger breeders put cocks in with hens for just a short time each day, but on a small scale this may not be practical. It is sometimes beneficial to trim the feathers around the vent to achieve maximum contact and therefore fertility.

**Utility aspects** Orpingtons have a strong tendency to go broody and make excellent mothers, being large enough to cover eggs of other species such as geese. Their own eggs are small and pinkish, the chicks taking longer than other breeds to feather up. There is certainly plenty of meat on this breed, but unless they are allowed to range the meat tends to be flabby. They mature at about two years old, but are greedy and run to fat very easily.

**Special requirements** Dry conditions and plenty of grass with lots of feed when growing and then restricted in adult life to keep them fit. Their small wings mean that they can usually be contained behind a low fence.

*Blue Orpington female.*

*Pair of black Orpingtons.*

*Mottled Pekin bantam female.*

# PEKIN BANTAM

*Standard colours*: black, blue (not laced), buff, cuckoo, mottled, barred, columbian,
   lavender, partridge, white
*True bantam, no large version*

**History** Looking like an animated teacosy, the Pekin was brought to Europe from China as loot when the Summer Palace at Pekin was destroyed during the Anglo-French expedition of 1860. They were originally thought to be miniatures of the Cochin, but it was decided that there are too many differences between the breeds for this to be correct. It is confusing when early books call them Cochin bantams and indeed in America they are still known by that name. The first colour imported was the buff and then other colours were produced together with profusion of the soft feathers, some colours in the UK and some in Europe, most notably the lavender in Holland.

**Current position** Adored by children, breeders and showmen, the Pekin bantam has universal appeal with both character and form.

**Characteristics** The tame and confiding nature of the Pekin makes it a wonderful first bantam for children, the birds happily riding round on a youngster's shoulder or accompanying them in almost any activity. Unfortunately this tameness does not extend to their own kind and the hens, particularly, can fight or boss strange hens around after separation. The abiding impression of a Pekin is roundness. Some say it should look like an inverted cup on a saucer. The plumage is very soft, long, abundant and wide and curls with the body lines. The tail is slightly higher than the head, leading to the typical Pekin tilt, plus a broad and low body with wide set legs showing no daylight under the body. The foot feather is profuse, growing from the outer and middle toes and is seen in the cocks as a fan around the feet. In the hens, the foot feather is often hidden by its fluff, as is the short tail hidden by the large cushion. The tail of the cocks is more obvious due to the long saddle feathers, but they are all still soft and without hard quills. The small single comb is erect and well serrated and the long earlobes and wattles are red.

The black has a beetle-green sheen with no white feathers and preferably dark undercolour, the blue is a pigeon blue with no lacing plus the male having a darker shade in the hackle, saddle and tail. The white is pure white and the buff must be an even shade throughout, right down to the skin. The sun fades buff colouring quicker than any other, so show birds are usually kept in the shade. The cuckoo has fuzzy bands of grey and dark grey across the feather, again, right down to the skin, and the barred is more definitely marked with bars of black across a white background, each feather finishing with a black tip and the bars going down to the skin. No other breed has both cuckoo and barred standardised as colours, probably due to the similarity to an untrained eye. The mottled is black, evenly mottled with a white tip to each feather. The good mottled pattern does not appear until the second year, and any bird which is rather too white in its first year (known as gay) will only increase the white as it gets older. The columbian is like the light Brahma with white body and black and white neck hackle, tail and wings. The lavender is a most beautiful and popular true-breeding colour comprising a pearl grey tint throughout. Never cross lavender with blue as both will be ruined. The partridge cock is similar to the partridge Wyandotte, with the hen brown (dead oak leaf shade) and pencilled all over with at least three concentric rings of glossy black on each feather. This is difficult to achieve all the way down to the feet. Legs in all colours are yellow, with dark shanks allowed in the black as long as the soles are yellow. Eyes are red in all colours.

**Utility aspects** Famous as broodies, the hens lay a clutch of about twelve and then sit. If they are broken off by being confined away from a nest for at least ten days they will lay again quite quickly, if eggs are needed rather than broodies. They are very attentive and protective mothers. Fertility can be affected by the profuse feathering around the vent, so trimming of this in the breeding season is recommended. In order to maintain the heavy foot feather, show birds are kept indoors on shavings or sand and only let onto grass occasionally. They can look rather anaemic if not often on grass, so greenery hung up in their pen and a log or two to give them exercise will keep them fit. Wet grass and damp conditions are not appreciated, but they are normally a robust and long lived fowl.

**Special requirements** Dry conditions and plenty of human company suit this charming little bantam.

*Partridge Pekin bantam female.*

*Black Pekin bantam female.*

# PLYMOUTH ROCK

*Standard colours*: barred, black, buff, columbian, white in large
*Bantam version:* yes (¼ size), large colours plus partridge, blue (not laced)

**History** This breed apparently had two goes at getting established. Firstly in an American publication of 1853 the Plymouth Rock is mentioned as a cross between Cochins, Dorkings, Malay and Jungle Fowl and, not surprisingly, the variation in plumage colour, leg colour and type was just as varied. By 1871 a completely different bird was called a Plymouth Rock, the previous effort considered by this time extinct, and this was the native American Dominique (a barred breed) crossed with Shanghais (early Cochins, also known as Javas, the latter, heavier type then going on to become a separate breed). Harrison Weir's drawing of one of the first Plymouth Rocks to come to Britain in 1856 shows the influence of both Dominique and an Asiatic breed, and eventually the barred pattern was established. The Canadians meanwhile had been busy creating their own version of this breed, concentrating most on the utility side, so there were slight differences in shape and colour between those and the exhibition birds. The buff Rock does not share the same parents as the barred, the buff being made by 1890 from buff Leghorn, buff Cochin and light Brahma, but selection

*Buff Plymouth Rock male.*

94

*Barred Plymouth Rock female.*

over time has made the type the same. The American Standard and The British Standard are not quite the same for the Plymouth Rock, but both are instantly recognisable in the flesh.

**Current position**  Rather more popular in the bantam than the large, but a pen of large barred Rock looks really smart and dapper. (Beware confusion with an excellent but badly named commercial free-range hybrid layer called Black Rock which is Plymouth Rock crossed with Rhode Island Red and comes in basic black with varying amounts of red in hackle and breast. This was developed in the States originally as Arbor Acres)

**Characteristics**  An upright and bold bird, well balanced with a large, deep and compact body. The back is broad, as is the breast and the wings are medium sized. The tail is medium with compact sickles and flowing saddle hackle in the male and small and compact in the female. The head is strong and bold with a medium upright single comb and the red earlobes are long and fine. The stance of a Plymouth Rock is square and strong and the yellow legs in all colours are a feature of the breed. Eyes are rich bay. The most famous colour is the barred Rock (the word Plymouth tends to be dropped when the colours are added). There is nothing to equal the sharply defined and smart look of a barred Rock, especially in the males. Each feather looks as though it has been drawn across with a narrow black pen and ruler. The ground colour is white with a bluish tinge and the barring is greeny-black and straight across, even in width with the ground colour and continuing right through to the skin, each feather finishing with a black tip. The barring in the female appears wider than that in the male. The buff Rock, mostly seen in bantam version, is an even golden buff down to the skin including the tail, as prone to fading in sunlight as other buff breeds and as difficult to get the colour even. The black has a beetle-green sheen and is rarely seen. The columbian has a white body with black vertically striped neck hackle, black tail which may be laced with white, black primaries (main wing feathers) and light slate undercolour which must not show through. The white is pure white. The bantam version has two extra colours standardised. The blue is an even, non-laced blue and the partridge, although similar in pattern to the partridge Wyandotte, is much redder in the hackle and back and a slight tinge of red is allowed on the black breast. The partridge Rock female has neck hackle of reddish bay with black centres and then each body feather has at least three concentric black pencillings conforming to the shape of the feather. Really good specimens are extremely difficult to achieve as there is so much which can go wrong with the pencilling.

**Utility aspects** Docile by nature and inclined to broodiness but originally developed as a dual purpose breed, utility strains of barred Rocks have retained their laying ability, producing light brown eggs at about 200 per year. The birds are long lived, not minding confinement and can be shown for several years. The exhibition strains are not as good layers, as a working bird never has the same perfection of feather and colour. It should be possible to have a happy medium, but this could be said of most breeds where man has determined to develop looks above usefulness. As a heavy breed, the Plymouth Rock cocks attain weights of 7½lb (3.4kg), but they are not as popular in the UK due to their yellow legs and skin. The Americans prefer yellow skin and the British prefer white skin on their table birds. The white Rock is one of the ancestors of the modern broiler. Chicks feather up and grow quickly and their docile nature makes them a good start for children, Juvenile classes being held at most major shows. Barred Rocks will throw the occasional all black bird.

**Special requirements** Vigorous and hardy, the Plymouth Rock needs extra vigilance on regular egg collecting to avoid too much broodiness.

# POLAND

*Standard colours*: chamois, gold, silver, self white, self black, self blue, white-crested black, white-crested blue, white-crested cuckoo

*Bantam version*: yes (¼ size)

**History** Birds with crests are mentioned in Aldrovandi's book on poultry of 1598 and they can be traced in Dutch paintings of the 1700s, long before punk hairstyles became fashionable. The origin of the name and the bird is still argued over, crested birds being described all over central Europe, not just in Poland, but most now agree that the name is derived from the enlarged poll (top of the head) supporting the crest. They had a classification at the first poultry show in London in 1845, proving their popularity then in four colours, including the laced ones. The old books seem slightly surprised that Polands breed so true and can be shown successfully for several years, although the crests have been improved, particularly in the cocks as photographs from the '30s reveal.

**Current position** Not only showman's birds, as they also lay well; they are much in demand for their outrageous looks and, with so many colours to choose from, a mixed flock in a garden seem like mobile flowers. The large version is not as numerous as the bantams.

**Characteristics** Having a Poland crest must be like permanently wearing a sombrero; they can see perfectly well forward and down, the best angle for feeding, but have restricted vision otherwise. This gives rise to the erroneous assumption that they are nervous – any hen spooks if it is surprised. They can be caught fairly easily just by creeping up on them

*White crested black Poland female.*

from behind, and they get very tame and confiding, particularly if you announce your presence by voice. This tends to make up for the fact that humans change their outer coverings in a most confusing way from the point of view of birds, which have good colour vision. The best stockmen tend to wear similar colours all the time and keep up a constant monologue when with their charges: anyone who thinks you are batty may not be wrong, but just isn't in tune with livestock.

Colours of the Polands are varied and spectacular. The most famous is probably the white-crested black with its black body and white crest with a black base line at the front. The other two similarly patterned colours are white-crested blue and white-crested cuckoo, although not so numerous. Confusingly, these three colours do not have a beard and have wattles and all the other colours have a beard with no wattles. The comb is minimal but if present should be of the horn type. Polands belong in the family of hens which have cavernous nostrils, most of which have a crest of some description such as Appenzeller, Houdan, Crévecoeur, La Flèche, plus white earlobes denoting a white egg. The crest should be perfectly round in the female with no split or twisted feathers. The male's crest is naturally more spiky due to the structure of the feathers, but should still maintain the globular shape. The bearded colours should have a bull neck, i.e. very abundant hackle, but in the non-bearded colours there is a finer outline. Eyes are red in all colours and beaks and legs are dark blue in all except the white-crested cuckoo where a paler beak and legs are allowed. The chamois, gold and silver varieties are laced. In the chamois this is white lacing around buff feathers, the gold is black lacing around golden-bay feathers and the silver is black lacing around silver feathers. The self colours are the same colour throughout and are not as popular, although a good white when well prepared for a show can be stunning. Some frizzled Polands have recently been imported from Holland, but not yet standardised. They are a novelty, but have a tendency to look merely untidy compared to Polands or Frizzles proper.

**Utility aspects** Despite their extraordinary looks Polands are good layers. They are classed as non-sitters, but do occasionally go broody. It is not wise to trust them as mothers until proven as they can be less than single-minded. Chicks are born with the shape of the crest in place, so culling can be done at this stage if necessary. The tops of their skulls are domed and soft, so care must be taken if kept with other breeds, or even too many Polands together, that they do not feather-peck the crests. Most breeders either cut the crests or tie them up so that they keep clean and have improved vision. For the best show specimens, not only does the crest have to be perfect, it has to be perfectly clean and they have this ingrained habit of getting said crest as dirty as possible if confined. If on free range the crest keeps much cleaner, but it is sensible to have drinkers with small access points. They are none too bright when it rains and will stand, dejectedly, getting wet from head to foot with their crests hanging down in ribbons. Due to their thin skulls they can get hypothermic easily, especially if there is a wind blowing as well. Vigilance is needed for lice and mites as Polands cannot easily preen their crests and lose condition very rapidly with Northern fowl mite, red mite or lice, the first two being potential killers.

**Special requirements** Dry conditions overhead, constant mite patrol and drinkers with small apertures will keep Polands looking good.

*Chamois Poland male.*

*White Poland female.*

# REDCAP

*Standard colours*: just the one original colour
*Bantam version*: no

**History**  Derbyshire Redcaps are considered a member of the Hamburgh family and carry some similarity of form and markings. They evolved in the hills of Derbyshire as a farmers' fowl, being very hardy, good layers and persistent foragers. They were used much in crossing programmes in the late 1870s, but gradually fell out of favour. Edward Brown says that but for the coarse comb it would doubtless have attained a much greater degree of popularity, with head points claiming 45 out of 100 judging points, still true today.

**Current position**  In very few hands, although there is a separate breed club, but Redcaps should really be considered as genuinely rare, needing more people to keep and breed them.

**Characteristics**  Redcaps are only happy when foraging away from people. They do not take kindly to being shown or confined and take every opportunity to escape. They are very self-reliant and sensible when out in the world and make an ideal hill bird. They are a well balanced shape with a full flowing tail carried at about 60°. The headgear is spectacular with a huge rose comb, flattened on top but with lots of tiny spikes, rather round in overall shape, carried well off the beak and eyes and set square on the head. Size in the male is about 3¼ in by 2¾ in (8.25 by 7cm) and about half that in the female. The eyes and earlobes are red with the legs lead colour. The neck and saddle hackle in the male has a red quill,

*Derbyshire Redcap male.*

100

beetle-green webbing and a fine fringe of black with a black tip. The back and shoulders are rich red tipped with black and the tail, breast and underparts are black. The hen has similar hackle to the cock but with a nut brown quill. Her ground colour is nut brown with half-moon black spangling on each feather and the tail black.

**Utility aspects** Excelling as a layer and forager, but with some meat potential as the cocks attain 6½lb (2.95kg). Although they range widely, the hens will usually use the henhouse in which to lay if the nestboxes are kept dark and private, being long lived and keeping in lay for many years. It was said that the eggs had a special flavour all their own: probably due to the large amount of greenery and invertebrates normally consumed. The chicks are vigorous and, somewhat surprisingly, bright yellow with black on the head and back when hatched. A certain amount of commercial feed is needed for Redcaps, but they love wheat and get much of their feed from foraging. When days are short or the weather really bad they deign to eat pellets, but care must be taken that a mineral supplement is added to the corn otherwise egg production will suffer. Mixed grit is also essential.

**Special requirements** Plenty of space to forage and as little confinement as possible and the Redcap will produce a large amount of eggs over several years.

# RHODE ISLAND RED

*Standard colours*: red
*Bantam version*: yes (¼ size)

**History**  The farmers of Narragansett Bay in the State of Rhode Island would probably be pleased to know that their efforts at creating a strong, vigorous and profitable fowl in the 1830s would make their area world famous. The birds then were not uniform, but they were red, and by the end of the century other crossings including red Malay, brown Leghorn and Cochin resulted in the Rhode Island Red. They were admitted to the American Standard in 1904, eggs having come to the UK the previous year. Star of the laying trials in the '30s, the Rhode Island Red was used in the '50s as the basis for the modern sex-linked hybrid battery hen. Exhibition birds have always been a darker red than utility strains, but there have probably been more nondescript cross bred brown chickens sold as Rhode Island Red as that was the only name people could remember.

**Characteristics**  'Rhodies' are classed as a heavy breed but are surprisingly active. They take confinement well, however, although liking to forage on grass. The body is broad and deep, oblong in shape. The back is broad and flat and the medium tail is carried well back, accentuating the length of the back. The broad breast is carried in a line perpendicular with the beak base, emphasising the brick shape. The head is carried slightly forward with a medium and upright broad based single comb. There is a rose comb version, seen mostly in the West Country nowadays. Earlobes are well developed and red, the prominent eyes are also red. Legs are yellow with a breeding cockerel showing red down the shanks. The red of the plumage is a rich, glossy, dark and lustrous red in the male, less glossy in the female. Undercolour is important and should be red or salmon. Too much attention to the dark colour has sometimes resulted in the feather structure suffering. The male should only have black in his wings and tail, the female has the same and can have black ticking at the base of her neck hackle as well.

**Utility aspects**  Rhodies were developed primarily as laying fowls, and their laying capacity has dominated the breed; they are still better than any other breed, taking consistent first prizes during the laying trials of the '30s. The modern poultry industry has much to thank the Rhode Island Red for due to its contribution to the production of worldwide cheap eggs in the form of the battery hybrid hen. If a laying strain can be obtained with the required dark red colour, and there are still some about, then utility and beauty is combined. Egg production should still be expected at 260 per year. The cocks weigh in at 8¼lb (3.85kg) so there is scope for meat production, but the yellow skin is not appreciated in the UK. The hens go broody in the right season, but are not permanently so. The chicks are vigorous and shades of gold when they hatch. Good quality feed and dry conditions suit this productive breed while growing.

The Rhode Island Red is genetically gold, so males crossed with genetically silver breeds such as Light Sussex females will give the famous sex-linked layer, so popular before the hybrids were developed. Genetic silver is found in white birds which have other plumage colours as well like silver laced Wyandotte, Sebright, columbian Wyandotte, light Brahma, etc. The colour crosses over the sex so that females are gold at dayold and males are silver. The genetics do not work as conveniently with the colour of the parents the other way round.

**Special requirements** Cull for any obvious defects such as roach back, knock knees or wall eyes (two white eyes).

*Rhode Island Red male.*

# ROSECOMB BANTAM

*Standard colours*: black, blue (not laced), white
*True bantam*: no large version

**History** Although the Victorian books mention the Rosecomb as an old breed of bantam, some have assumed in those times that it was a miniature of the black Hamburg, sharing the same style comb and tail, but the body and type are very different. Rosecombs enjoyed a certain amount of notoriety for many years as a breed that was manufactured rather than bred, in other words exhibitors were faking colouring and feathers. It must have been tempting if a really cracking bird had damaged an earlobe, say, to whiten the damaged part. Judges were only too aware of what was going on and eventually the practices were officially banned. Faking nowadays is also banned but it is a clever and experienced judge who can spot modern methods done well or count feathers if he thinks some are missing, especially for the top awards. There is a fine dividing line between faking and show preparation, however. The Rosecomb has always been considered entirely an exhibition bird, although it lays quite well.

**Current position** Very popular among the showing fraternity, but with the limited range of colours available, people tend to chose more colourful breeds.

**Characteristics** With its jaunty and important carriage, the Rosecomb turns heads wherever it is seen. The comb from which it is named carries 20 points out of 100, so the square, well filled front tapering to the long straight leader is a dominant feature in the breeding pen. The spotlessly white earlobe, most striking in the black, is perfectly round and with uniform thickness, not dished or hollow and kid-glove-like in texture. Size in the standard is in ¾ -⅞in (1.88-2.19cm) in the males, but this is generally exceeded in show birds. The face must be red with no white in it at all, the eyes are hazel in the black and red in the white and the wattles are round, neat and fine. The body is cobby but not dumpy and has a short back with a lovely sweeping curve from neck to sickles. The shoulders are broad and flat and the breast is carried well up and has a bold curve around the front. Wings are carried on the low side, obscuring part of the thighs and the stern is also broad, not running down to a heart shape like the Old English Game. Legs are short, emphasising the cobby shape. The tail is an important feature, particularly in the cocks with feathers being very broad and round ended instead of the more normal pointed cock feathers, the whole effect being one of flowing gracefulness. A couple of ounces larger than the Dutch, the Rosecomb cock weighs in at 22oz (620g), the hen four ounces less. The black has a beautiful green sheen with black legs, the white is pure white with white legs and the blue is a medium blue with no lacing and dark blue legs. In Australia and America there are other colours standardised such as brown-red and cuckoo.

**Utility aspects** The hens are quite good layers, the eggs being very small, but the chicks can be rather weedy and need extra care for the first few weeks with warm and dry conditions, no competition from other birds and high quality chick crumbs. The hens are not top-class broodies and most breeders artificially incubate and rear the chicks, thereby being more in control of the critical first weeks. Once reared, the Rosecomb is hardy.

**Special requirements** Extra care with young chicks and generally dry conditions are needed. In northern climates, beware frostbite on the comb and leader.

*Black Rosecomb bantam male.*

*White Rosecomb bantam male.*

# SCOTS DUMPY

*Standard colours*: no fixed plumage colour, but colours most seen are cuckoo, black, with
   white, brown, gold and silver rarely available and not as typey
*Bantam version*: yes (¼ size)

**History**  It seems improbable that cattle and poultry can share a genetic trait but the dwarfing gene which makes the Dexter short-legged also created the main feature of the Scots
Dumpy. Aristotle and Pliny both mention dwarf poultry with praise as to their productivity
and they distinguish small (bantam) from short-legged (dwarf). Aldrovandi (1598) writes of
chickens creeping over the earth, limping rather than walking, which exactly describes the
waddling gait of the Scots Dumpy. This particular genetic feature of short legs in poultry
thus has great antiquity, but the Scots Dumpy is first mentioned by name in the 1850s, being
exhibited in 1852 in London. Authors of books at the time failed to find more birds in
Scotland to prolong the novelty although the birds were reputed to have been kept in Scotland from time immemorial, unfortunately undocumented. They were supposed to be the
fowl which the Romans hated as they always alerted the Picts and Scots to any approaching
danger, but it is well known that all armies had the habit of carrying cockerels with them as
alarm clocks and time keepers. Dumpies were also known, not only in Scotland but in
Europe, as 'Creepers' or 'Bakies'.

**Current position**  Although they have their devotees and recently their own breed club, the
numbers of Scots Dumpies have swung widely over the years, probably due to the wastage
when breeding and problems with infertility. The addition of new colours when the original
colours are in such low numbers seems merely to confuse people.

*Black Scots Dumpy male.*
*RIGHT Pair of Scots Dumpy, cuckoo male, black female.*

**Characteristics** Most obviously, the short legs, the shank of which should not exceed 1½in (3.75cm), and this gives them their characteristically waddling gait. They are wide and heavy bodied with a long back and a full and flowing tail, the sickles well arched. The head is neat with a medium sized single comb, red earlobes and red eyes. The black has a lovely beetle-green sheen with dark legs and the cuckoo has fuzzy bands of grey and dark grey across each feather with white mottled legs. They are sensible birds, but feeding needs to avoid maize as they can easily get too fat on it, which restricts their movements still further and gives them liver problems. The short legged gene has a lethal factor, so when breeding there is wastage of birds which are dead in the shell, plus the problem that only a percentage of birds hatch with short legs, the others having normal legs.

**Utility aspects** With such short legs, they need easy terrain to thrive on, but make excellent and docile broodies; gamekeepers in Scotland used nothing else for years. The birds that turn out long legged can be used for layers (tinted eggs) as they lay well, or for meat, but in the breeding pen it is better to use all short legged birds. The chicks are reasonably easy to rear as long as their short stature is taken into account with drinkers and feeders. Do not let them onto wet grass too early as they will chill, being so close to the ground. It is not often that you see adult cocks reach their standard weight of 7lb (3.2kg), but they still carry plenty of flesh.

**Special requirements** Scots Dumpies need to be kept dry as chicks, fattening foods restricted as adults and they do like to free range.

# SCOTS GREY

*Standard colours:* barred
*Bantam version:* yes (¼ size)

**History** It is hardly surprising that the nation that invented the tartan should develop a breed of poultry that is hard-wearing, versatile, striped and chequered, albeit in a limited range of colours, with 'Shepherd's Plaid' being one colloquial name. About the only fact the Victorian poultry books agree on is that the Scots Grey is a very old breed, going back to the sixteenth century. Its shape was probably similar to the long-legged, upright stance required today, devotees having avoided the Victorian passion of adding a meaty breed to expand the quantity. It was known primarily as a cottagers' fowl, the hens partaking of warmth and light from the hearth in the winter and laying large cream coloured eggs. The Scots Grey Club was one of the earliest formed in 1885 and although most birds are still kept in Scotland, the Sassenachs are learning to appreciate the qualities of this hardy breed.

*Scots Grey male*

**Current position** There will always be those who need a hardy breed in the harsher climes and the dapper Scots Grey has proved itself over many centuries. The bantam version is popular with children as they become tame easily and do well in shows. Members of the Royal Scots Grey regiment, when not serving abroad, have made a point of keeping Scots Greys, but it is still a sadly neglected breed.

**Characteristics** This breed is revered for its hardiness and ability to thrive in any climatic conditions, laying a large egg for the size of bird, only 5lb (2.25kg) in the adult hen. It is a very active breed and likes to range widely, getting many additions to its diet from foraging. A good commercial diet is needed to balance the nutrition, especially when it is too cold for invertebrates to be plentiful or daylight hours short. There is but one colour and pattern in the Scots Grey and that is barred. Other breeds having this colour have barred in their names, such as Barred Plymouth Rock, Barred Wyandotte and Barred Pekin. It can be mistakenly called cuckoo by the inexperienced, but this pattern is a sharp, well defined, equal width barring of alternate steel grey and black going across the body, thigh and wing feathers, but in a 'V' on the neck hackle, saddle and tail in the males. The females have wider barring and really do look like grey tartan. The colour in both sexes should 'read' throughout, i.e. the same from head to tail. The single comb is medium sized, earlobes red and the eyes are amber. Beaks are white with black streaks and legs are white with black mottles. The standard states that a bird should be disqualified from showing if any characteristic of any other breed not applicable to the Scots Grey is evident, such is the confidence that the Scots Grey is unique. Birds destined for showing should be kept out of strong sunlight as this makes the feathers go brassy, much frowned upon.

**Utility aspects** This is an unimproved dual purpose breed, developed over hundreds of years, laying well on mostly foraging, plus having room for succulent meat on the tall and rangy body. The breast is carried high but is also deep, and the thighs are prominent. The chicks hatch readily and mature quickly, important in northern regions with short summers. Classed as a non-sitter, the hens will occasionally go broody but do not like to be disturbed. They will rear chicks efficiently and teach them to forage, but artificially reared ones definitely have the foraging instinct.

**Special requirements** With their long legs and active natures, Scots Greys prefer to range, often roosting in trees, but most poultry keepers provide suitable housing for the safety of the birds.

# SEBRIGHT BANTAM

*Standard colours*: gold, silver
*True bantam, no large version*

**History**  The Sebright is a truly British breed, created during the early 1800s by Sir John Sebright. When other breeders were trying to breed down the large breeds to obtain pigmies, or bantams as they later became known, Sir John decided to produce something new. Apart from the lacing, then seen on Polands, the feathering of the Sebright is strange in that the cocks have the same rounded feathers as the hens. Sir John used Nankin, henny Game and gold spangled Hamburgh. The Nankin was for the ground colour, described when mixed with the others and fixed as 'the beautiful tint of the inside of the shell of a Jordan almond', a particular golden-bay shade. The henny Game was for the hen feathering on the cocks, and although Lewis Wright complains bitterly that the fertility was permanently affected by this, the henny Game is most prolific, and Harrison Weir suggests that fertility problems were created because only the smallest and puniest specimens were used to breed with, which makes sense. The gold spangled Hamburgh, when crossed with the Game produced the lacing, so the gold was the first colour and the silver was created from it later. Breeders of Sebrights spent many years perfecting the ground colour and lacing of these attractive birds, entries at shows being consistently high. The silver was used to create the lacing in silver laced Wyandottes in the late 1800s (see Wyandotte). In other countries the citron Sebright (yellow ground colour) is standardised as well.

**Current position**  Very popular due to their attractive lacing, but not as numerous as some other breeds as they are not a beginner's bird, being not very fertile, not very hardy and subject to stress.

*Silver Sebright bantam female.*

**Characteristics**  As mentioned earlier, the ground colour of the gold is a golden-bay and there is glossy green-black lacing around each feather, the high tail included, on both cocks and hens, those on the body being almond shaped, giving an embossed appearance. It is not easy to get a clear ground colour and the black lacing; pepperiness (spotting on the ground colour) and rusty lacing is often passed off as a gold Sebright. The silvers have the same well defined lacing, but with a silver-white ground colour. Undercolour is slate in both colours. The original Sebrights had gipsy faces, i.e. dark mulberry-coloured skin, but this is now rarely seen in the hens and almost unobtainable in the cocks. The eye should be dark in both colours. The comb is rose, square-fronted with a leader which is slightly turned up, the earlobes are red and the clean legs slate-blue. The whole carriage is strutting and tremulous, on tiptoe, leading the Victorians to call it an impertinent stance, the cock weighing only 22oz (620g). The neck of the cock is held leaning backwards, but that of the hen is upright. The back is very short with a prominent breast and low wing carriage. These highly strung birds become tame with handling, but the hens will fight to the death after they have been separated or a strange hen introduced.

**Utility aspects**  Compatibility of pairs seems an important aid to fertility, with May being the best time to breed. As with all true bantams, incubation is usually 20 days. If the eggs are fertile, the chicks are reasonably vigorous, but keep them separate from other breeds, dry underfoot and with high quality chick crumbs until they are at least 14 weeks old. They are prone to Marek's disease, a herpes virus in the environment which attacks the peripheral nerves in the legs and wings, making them useless. It is quite easy and cheap to vaccinate against this.

**Special requirements**  Good rearing facilities which must be dry; suitably sized drinkers and feeders and vaccination against Marek's is needed, together with the space to breed with pairs rather than more than one hen. Not a beginner's breed.

*Gold Sebright bantam male.*

# SILKIE

*Standard colours*: black, blue, gold, white, partridge
*Bantam version*: yes (¼ size)

**History**  The intrepid explorer Marco Polo in the 13th century mentioned fowl with wool instead of feathers in his travels in India, China and Japan. No-one is certain where the Silkie originated, but Aldrovandi wrote of them in 1645 as having hair like a cat; the first specimens imported to the UK were from India in about 1850. They immediately won hearts with their perennial broodiness and unusual looks. People still talk of the Silkie bantam as though it was one word: it is not a bantam, but a light breed of large fowl and used extensively for crossing with other breeds to produce more broodies. Very recently, a bantam version has been created.

**Current position**  Now with both large and bantam version, the maternal Silkie is even more popular. They are more cuddly than most other hens and so children get on well with them.

**Characteristics**  Fluffy maternal stoutness is the first impression, but they are lively and busy when not on duty. The feathers have no webbing and so are soft and silky, even the wing and short tail feathers being ragged. With no possibility of flight, Silkies can be kept behind very low fencing, doing little damage in the garden in any case. The male has an almost circular mulberry coloured comb with a dent across the middle and the wattles are

*White Silkie female.*

also mulberry. Red in the face and comb is a serious defect. The earlobes are a surprising turquoise blue, but small and round in the female, more oval in the male. The crest in the male is soft and full with about a dozen soft, longer feathers streaming gracefully backwards for about 1½in (3.7cm). The female has a broad and 'Cochiny' saddle and tail and apparently very short legs. The crest is short and neat like a circular powder puff, with a very small comb. Eyes are brilliant black in all colours and the beak is slaty blue. The short legs are lead colour with five toes and moderate feathering on the shank, down to the outer and middle toes. Any green in the legs is frowned upon. Colours in the Silkie are mainly self because with unstructured feathers, markings have little shape. The white is snow white and the black has a green sheen in the males with a little colour in the hackle permissible but not desirable. The blue is an even shade of blue from head to tail and is a difficult colour to maintain as with successive breedings the colour tends to fade and turns out an unattractive dirty grey. The gold is a bright shade throughout and darker tails in both sexes are permitted. The partridge has recently been admitted to the Standard: in the male it is a mixture of orange and black and in the female, the crest, neck and breast is lemon striped with black with the rest of the body a soft partridge brown with black barring. The bearded Silkie, the same as the above but with beard and muffs, is popular on the Continent and in America.

*Black Silkie male.*

*Gold Silkie male.*

**Utility aspects**  Most feather-legged breeds are inclined to broodiness and are not good layers. The Silkie is famous for its seeming ability to mother anything, but like all breeds, individuals will vary. The egg is small and pinkish with production at not much more than 100 a year, but given good food and shelter in the winter when every sensible chicken's hormones are shut down with the short days, the Silkie starts to lay about Christmas. She will produce a clutch of about 10 eggs and, even if they are taken away, will go broody. They are liable to stop laying altogether in the summer, so it is as well to take advantage of the early broodiness. Some of the exhibition strains are rather highly strung, so if broodiness is the prime requirement, make sure the hens are from a good broody strain.

Some Silkies do not mind being moved to a special broody place, but to be sure (and this applies to other breeds as well), take a cardboard box to her with shavings or straw in it. Place her gently in this with any eggs she is on, preferably at night, and let her settle in the box with the lid closed: darkness is a great calming influence. Then, after an hour or so, take her to her broody box and gently transfer her, plus eggs, and leave her in the dark. If you walk about with her under your arm in broad daylight she may understandably go off the brooding idea. The next day, take her off the nest for feeding, watering and a large defecation, making sure she goes back in about 20 minutes, but do not hassle her. Only when this routine is established over a few days is it safe to put the eggs you want hatched under her. Some broodies can be trusted to get off the nest every day on their own, but others can starve themselves and go into a complete trance. It is important that she is separate from the other hens so that they cannot lay unwanted eggs under her. If several broodies are in the same area, try and make sure that they are going to hatch at the same time, because if they hear cheeping, they will assume those doing so are their own chicks and leave their nest to go to them. Otherwise keep broodies in separate boxes as they will fight over the number of eggs available. If you want to foster chicks, they need to be added within the first 24 hours of any other hatchings preferably of different colours. Hens have colour vision and form a sort of photographic picture of their chicks within this time. Fortunately they cannot count, so if different coloured chicks are added to an already motley collection, it should be successful. Otherwise extras are regarded as intruders and likely to get killed.

White Silkies can be used as a sex-linked cross with any silver hen as the white Silkie is genetically gold (see Autosexing). This is very useful on, say, light Sussex, as the ginger coloured subsequent hens make more weatherproof and larger broodies, the feathers on pure Silkies sometimes getting wrapped round the neck of a chick with fatal consequences.

The Chinese seem to consider the Silkie a culinary delicacy, but their black skin and flesh takes some getting used to. Surplus Silkie cockerels have no market whatsoever, attaining weights of 4lb (1.8kg), and there always seem to be more of them than hens, it only being possible to sex them with accuracy after fifteen weeks old, the usual feather sexing of pointed in males and rounded in females being useless with no feather structure.

**Special requirements**  Dry conditions at all times as the feathers are not waterproof. Separate brooding accommodation if possible. Very susceptible to scaly leg (a burrowing irritant mite, cured with surgical spirit). Also susceptible to Marek's disease (see Sebright).

# SUSSEX

*Standard colours*: brown, buff, light, red, speckled, silver, white
*Bantam version*: yes (¼ size)

**History** Part of the Victorian craze for poultry was, not unnaturally, the eating of them, and the Old Sussex or Kent fowls were considered with the Dorking to be the finest of them all. With a Sussex breed club formed in 1903, development continued as a dual purpose breed with several distinctive colours created. The original colours were brown, red and speckled. The light, probably the most famous colour, was made from the light Brahma, Cochin and silver grey Dorking and then went on to excel in all the laying trials of the '30s, despite being classed as a heavy breed. Buffs appeared around 1920 and whites shortly after that. The silver is the latest variety. The light was used in the 1930s in sex-linkage experiments with the Rhode Island Red, Rhode cocks, being genetically gold, producing gold female chicks off genetically silver light Sussex hens, male chicks being silver (see Autosexing section). These went on, after much selection and the addition of white Leghorn, to become the brown battery hybrid hen of today. The modern broiler is a product of the Sussex and Indian Game, so the breed has made an immense contribution to the poultry industry as well as being a popular backyard breed.

**Current position** Kept either as an exhibition bird or a dual purpose utility bird, the only colours in few hands are the browns and the reds, the rarer colours. Light Sussex, particularly bantams, regularly take top honours at shows.

**Characteristics** One of the most famous and productive breeds of poultry, the docile Sussex are quite happy free ranging or being more confined. They are graceful with a long and broad flat back, the tail at an angle of 45° and a fine and neat head with a medium sized erect single comb. The brown is not an exciting colour, being dark brown in the male with

*Speckled Sussex female.*

117

black points and paler brown in the female with black points: the red is a richer colour. The other colours are not only more popular, they are more spectacular. The light has a stark contrast of white neck striped with black, white body and black wings and tail. The buff has ginger where the light has white and is a pleasing combination, needing to be kept out of the sun due to fading of the colour if showing. The white is pure white throughout, but the speckled is a lovely mixture of mahogany, black and white, in that order, on each feather, more white coming through as the bird moults each year. The silver has the same neck as the light, but the body is black with silver lacing and white shafts to the feathers, reminiscent of chain mail. Eyes are red in the darker colours and orange in the lighter colours, earlobes red and legs white in all colours.

**Utility aspects** An extremely good layer in the light and white varieties, the other colours not as good. Any of the colours will produce fine carcases. The eggs are large and cream to light brown in colour, equalling the Rhode Island Red in numbers per year. The chicks are strong and mature quite quickly for a heavy breed. The speckled are the slowest maturing and the most likely to go broody, being large enough to cover other eggs such as geese with ease. Weights of cocks should be 9lb (4.1kg) minimum and in the '30s, the brown cocks were said to reach 14lb (6.3kg). The difficulty with utility and exhibition birds is that for an exhibition bird to be at its best with plenty of 'bloom', especially in the hens, it should be just about to lay, not having spent the past few months being a properly productive Sussex, so birds tend to be hatched so that their coming into lay coincides with a certain show, knowing that the following year, the bird will be useless for showing but very productive. This method is preferable to selecting birds which do not lay well and merely look beautiful, doing the breed no good at all.

**Special requirements** Sussex are relatively easy and adaptable, but they do need good quality food to attain their potential.

*Trio of Silver Sussex.*
*RIGHT Quintet of Light Sussex females.*

# WELSUMMER

*Standard colours*: gold partridge (black-red), silver duckwing
*Bantam version*: yes (¼ size)

**History**  In the *Feathered World Yearbook* of 1936 the Welsummer Club members and exhibitors were told in no uncertain terms to make up their minds what they wanted as plumage colour or otherwise leave the birds at home. The first eggs of this Dutch breed were brought to England in the 1920s. In the beginning the eggs were thought to be a hoax as the deep terracotta colouring can be scrubbed off. The breed was developed near the town of Welsum using a mixture of Partridge Cochin, Partridge Wyandotte, Barnevelder, Rhode Island Red, Croad Langshan and Partridge Leghorn and the object was to obtain as deep a coloured egg as possible, so the plumage to start with was not considered important. Hence the exasperated exhortation above. A bantam version was certainly in existence in the '30s, but again with tremendous variation in plumage.

**Current position**  The gorgeous colouring of the cockerel allied to the terracotta eggs makes this breed endlessly popular, there never seeming to be enough pullets available to satisfy demand. Being able to show both the birds and the eggs gives an extra angle to exhibiting.

**Characteristics**  Classed in its native Holland as a medium breed, we have just heavy and light classifications in the UK and at present the Welsummer is in the light class. It is certainly one of the heaviest light breeds, but is upright in carriage and alert and active. The latter quality needs working on rather like the Marans as the Welsummer will get lazy and fat, given the chance, not minding confinement. A fat bird is not a productive bird. The body is well built with the back broad and long, the breast full and well rounded. The full tail is carried high, but beware of squirrel tail (tail too close to head). In accordance with the utility emphasis the abdomen is long, deep and wide. The medium single comb is upright and the earlobes are red. When this breed is exhibited, the judge must take into account the 'indications of productiveness' which carry 30 points out of the 100, so birds must be fit and compact. The colour of the Welsummer is the classic storybook colouring in the male of orange and black from a distance, but close up golden-brown neck and saddle hackle, back, shoulders and wing bow bright red-brown. The rest of the body is black, excepting the breast and underparts, which are red mottled. The female has golden brown hackle with black striping and a golden shaft. The breast is a rich chestnut-red continuing to the thighs with the back and wing bow reddish brown, each feather peppered with black specks, (partridge marking), the shaft of the feather showing bright and very distinct. The tail is black with the outer feathers pencilled with brown. The silver duckwing was a sport from the normal colour and is similar to the silver grey Dorking but with white in the wings and tail. In both colours the eyes are red and the legs yellow with slate grey undercolour.

**Utility aspects**  The Welsummer is supposed to be a non-sitter; they do sometimes go broody, but are not very good mothers. It is the wonderful colour of large egg that attracts people, erroneously thinking that a brown egg is tastier, healthier, fresher even than a white one. The Americans will only have white eggs in their commercial units because they can see that they are clean. Production is about 200 per year and if pushed to do more, the colour tends to go from the egg. The matt brown pigment is added last in the sequence of egg-making from a gland near the end of the oviduct and can be removed by scrubbing. The colour docs vary between individual hens and some add speckles to the dark colour. Depending on the stage in that particular laying cycle, the colour can fade or go darker. If purchasing eggs for setting it is best to go for the darkest ones. Cocks should get to 7lb (3.2kg) and have plenty of meat on them, but are usually easy to place in other homes if necessary due to the colouring.

The chicks are strong and have the added advantage that the females have much darker and better defined head and back markings at dayold. Using this, the accuracy of sexing is about 90%. Eggs do well at shows if they are of good shape, colour and freshness. Not all the bantams produce the same colour egg as the large version.

**Special requirements** Make sure that setting eggs are as dark as possible or if buying birds that their eggs are seen to be the right colour.

*Welsummer male.*

# WYANDOTTE

*Standard colours:* barred, black, blue (not laced), buff, columbian, partridge, silver pencil-
    led, red, white, silver laced, gold laced, blue laced, buff laced
*Bantam version*: yes (¼ size)

**History** People tend to have difficulty with the title of this breed, named after a tribe of
North American Indians. It should be pronounced 'Why-an-dot', but other offerings range
from 'Wine-dot' through to 'Win-an-dottie', reminiscent of a music hall act. As in much
vaudeville, the Wyandotte is not an original, being created in America from many breeds
during the 1800s including Hamburg, Sebright (for the lacing), Brahma and Cochin. The
silver laced was the first colour to be standardised in 1883 and some birds were imported to
England shortly after, amongst great publicity. The Victorians were inordinately fond of
their poultry and vied constantly to produce the biggest and the best. This is reflected in the
books of the time which were less than accurate on some breeds if the author did not like
them. One of the earlier importers was a Mr Spencer from Gloucestershire who had great
success with a particular cockerel. Eventually the bird died and was stuffed and kept in a
glass case in the bird room. His son, A.J. Spencer, became one of the leading silver laced
Wyandotte breeders in the country, showing and judging until shortly before his death in
1987 at the age of 86, the stuffed cockerel still keeping an eye on standards. Every subsequent colour was created by a different mix of breeds and it is interesting that the Columbian
was so named as it was first exhibited in 1893 at the Columbia Exposition or World Fair
held in Chicago: the plumage pattern is now known genetically as the columbian pattern in
any breed (see Brahma, Plymouth Rock, Sussex). Different utility and exhibition strains
gradually evolved in the white as the former was a useful layer and meat bird and the latter
just a beautiful ball of fluff.

**Current position** The laced and pencilled varieties are the most popular as they are very
attractive. The breed is still a useful dual purpose one and the bantams as numerous as the large.

**Characteristics** Docile in nature, the Wyandotte is a breed of curves. The breast is full,
broad and round and the back broad and short with a full and broad saddle rising with a
concave sweep to the medium sized rather upright tail. The head is short and broad with the
small rose comb closely following the line of the skull and neck. The clean legs are yellow
in all thirteen colours and the eyes are bright bay. The beak is also yellow, but can shade to
horn in the laced varieties and darker in the black. Earlobes are red. The whites are
extremely popular with exhibitors and regularly take top honours at shows, but there are
now very few utility whites. The silver laced always takes the eye with its clear silver ground
colour, each feather surrounded by a fine black line. The other laced colours are gold laced,
where silver is replaced by a rich golden bay, blue laced with ground colour red-brown and
blue lacing (very attractive) and buff laced with ground colour buff and white lacing. It can
be confusing when the names are not consistent with the ground colour and lacing. There
are two pencilled varieties, the partridge and the silver pencilled. The partridge in the male
is orange-yellow striped with black on the neck and saddle hackle, red on the shoulders and
back with bay on the wings, black elsewhere. The female has a wonderful pattern all over of
three fine black lines on each feather, following the feather outline and on a soft, light
partridge brown background. Problems occurring with this difficult pattern are mossy
(blotchy) background, broken pencilling and light shafts to the breast feathers. The black

tail is hidden by the pencilled coverts (covering feathers). The silver pencilled is similar in pattern to the partridge but silver-white in the male instead of yellow and red and steel-grey in the female instead of brown. The barred is similar to the barred Plymouth Rock, the black has a beetle-green sheen and the blue is a medium even blue, free of lacing. The buff suffers from the usual problems of fading in sunlight and difficulty of getting an all over even colour and the columbian is similar to the light Brahma with white body, black and white neck and tail and slate undercolour. The latest colour to be made, the red, was standardised in 1938 and is similar to the Rhode Island Red except the Wyandotte has black in the neck hackle in the male.

When exhibiting, the scale of points differs between the laced and pencilled varieties and the others as more points are awarded for the patterning of the former.

**Utility aspects** All the colours of Wyandottes lay reasonably well with the exception of the top exhibition strains. The egg is tinted and rather rounded. With all the various other breeds in their make-up, there is plenty of hybrid vigour, so the chicks are strong and grow quite quickly for a heavy breed. The cocks weigh a minimum of 9lb (4.8kg) but with the yellow skin they are not as popular in the UK for eating as white skinned birds. The bantams have a maximum weight of 3¾lb (1.7kg) in the males. The nature of the Wyandotte is docile and the hens make good broodies but like most breeds they are difficult to break off unless you specifically want to move them elsewhere (see Silkie).

**Special requirements** Even as pets, go for the best you can obtain, especially in the laced and pencilled varieties. Beware of knock knees in some strains.

*Partridge Wyandotte female.*

123

*White Wyandotte female.*

*Blue laced Wyandotte female.*

*Barred Wyandotte female.*

# Appendix I
# COMPLETE CLASSIFICATION OF BREEDS

## SOFT FEATHER: heavy

Australorp
Barnevelder
Brahma
Cochin
Croad Langshan
Dorking
Faverolles
Frizzle
Marans
Orpington
Plymouth Rock
Rhode Island Red
Sussex
Wyandotte

## SOFT FEATHER: light

Ancona
Appenzeller
Araucana
Rumpless Araucana
Hamburgh
Leghorn
Minorca
Poland
Redcap
Scots Dumpy
Scots Grey
Silkie
Welsummer

## HARD FEATHER

Asil (Rare)
Belgian Game (Rare)
Indian Game
Ko-Shamo (Rare)
Malay (Rare)
Modern Game
Nankin-Shamo (Rare)
Old English Game Bantam
Old English Game Carlisle
Old English Game Oxford
Rumpless Game (Rare)
Shamo (Rare)
Tuzo (Rare: True Bantam)
Yamato-Gunkei (Rare)

## TRUE BANTAM

Belgian
Booted (Rare)
Dutch
Japanese
Nankin (Rare)
Pekin
Rosecomb
Sebright
Tuzo (Hard Feather: Rare)

# RARE

## HARD FEATHER:

Asil
Belgian Game
Ko-Shamo Bantam
Malay
Nankin-Shamo Bantam
Rumpless Game
Shamo
Tuzo (True Bantam)
Yamato-Gunkei

## SOFT FEATHER: heavy

Autosexing Breeds: Rhodebar
                       Wybar
Crèvecoeur
Dominique
German Langshan
Houdan
Ixworth
Jersey Giant
La Flèche
Modern Langshan
New Hampshire Red
Norfolk Grey
North Holland Blue
Orloff
Transylvanian Naked Neck
Turkeys

## SOFT FEATHER: light

Andalusian
Augsberger
Autosexing Breeds: Legbar
                             Welbar
Brakel
Breda
Campine
Fayoumi
Friesian
Italiener
Kraienköppe
Lakenvelder
Marsh Daisy
Old English Pheasant Fowl
Sicilian Buttercup
Spanish
Sulmtaler
Sultan
Sumatra
Vorwerk
Yokohama

## TRUE BANTAM

Booted
Nankin
Tuzo (Hard Feather)

# Appendix 2
# GUIDE TO PURE BREED LAYING CAPABILITIES

| Breed | Egg colour | Numbers p.a | Maturing | Type |
|---|---|---|---|---|
| Ancona | white | 200 | quick | light |
| Andalusian | white | 200 | medium | light |
| Araucana | blue/green | 150 | quick | light |
| Australorp | tinted | 180 | medium | heavy * |
| Barnevelder | light brown | 180 | medium | heavy |
| Brahma | tinted | 150 | slow | heavy * |
| Cochin | tinted | 100 | slow | heavy * |
| Croad Langshan | brownish | 180 | medium | heavy * |
| Dorking | white | 190 | medium | heavy * |
| Faverolles | tinted | 180 | medium | heavy * |
| Fayoumi | tinted | 250 | quick | light |
| Friesian | white | 230 | quick | light |
| Frizzle | tinted | 175 | medium | heavy |
| Hamburg | white | 200 | quick | light |
| Indian Game | tinted | 100 | medium | heavy |
| Leghorn | white | 240 | quick | light |
| Marans | brown | 200 | medium | heavy * |
| Minorca | white | 200 | medium | light |
| Old English Game | tinted | 200 | quick | heavy * |
| Old E. Pheasant Fowl | white | 200 | quick | light |
| Orpington | tinted | 190 | medium | heavy * |
| Plymouth Rock | tinted | 200 | medium | heavy |
| Poland | white | 200 | quick | light |
| Derbyshire Redcap | tinted | 200 | quick | light |
| Rhode Island Red | tinted/brown | 260 | medium | heavy |
| Scots Dumpy | tinted | 180 | medium | heavy * |
| Scots Grey | tinted | 200 | quick | light |
| Silkie | tinted | 150 | quick | light  * |
| Sussex | tinted | 260 | medium | heavy |
| Welsummer | brown | 200 | medium | heavy |
| Wyandotte | tinted | 200 | medium | heavy |

* most likely to go broody

Some colour varieties of breeds lay better than others, and different exhibition and utility strains exist.

# USES OF SOME BREEDS

BREEDS PARTICULARLY SUITABLE FOR FREE RANGE
Ancona
Barnevelder
Belgian bantam
Fayoumi
Hamburgh
Leghorn
Marans
Minorca
Scots Dumpy
Old English Pheasant Fowl
Derbyshire Redcap

BREEDS PARTICULARLY GOOD FOR MEAT
Andalusian
Cochin
Croad Langshan
Dorking
Faverolles
Indian Game
Marans
Modern Game
Old English Game
Old English Pheasant Fowl
Orpington
Rhode Island Red
Scots Grey
Sussex
Welsummer
Wyandotte

BREEDS FOR CHILDREN
Barnevelder
Pekin bantam
Plymouth Rock
Scots Grey bantam
Silkie

BREEDS SUITABLE FOR CONFINEMENT
Any feather legged breed
Araucanas
Leghorn
Minorca
Modern Game
Plymouth Rock
Welsummer

BREEDS FOR BEGINNERS
Barnevelder
Belgian bantam
Cochin
Croad Langshan
Marans
Rhode Island Red
Light Sussex
Welsummer

# Appendix 3
# SHOW PREPARATION

This does not just mean having clean birds. Show preparation starts months before a show because fitness (correct feeding for good bone and muscle) is the framework upon which all the superficial items such as feathers are built. With some early maturing breeds it is only possible to show them in their first year, which usually means just coming into lay, so that hatching has to be timed to match point of lay (usually 18 weeks) and the chosen show(s). This effectively means that if these breeds do not have all the breed points when they are young, they are unlikely ever to have them. Other breeds do not mature until they are at least two years old, so will gain in breadth of body if the frame is there as youngsters.

Even dark coloured birds need washing for a show. Either washing-up liquid or baby shampoo is normally used. The birds are dunked in warm water, lathered, rinsed and dried either in front of a fire or with a hair drier. They rather like this. It is best to wash birds at least a week before a show to allow the natural body oils to return to the feathers. Put the birds in a clean show pen in an area with lots of human activity to get them used to the bustle of a show. If the birds are tame as well, then so much the better. Don't forget the legs which may need scrubbing gently and ingrained dirt gently removing from under the scales with a wooden toothpick. Those feather colours which are liable to fade or change in strong sunshine tend to be kept in outdoor runs which are covered over, which means they are still fit and still the correct colour. If you must wash a bird the day before a show, make sure it is dry before you box it as otherwise the feathers will stick out at all angles. Always try and use boxes that are too big so that the birds have enough room both to keep cool and to turn around which protects the tail feathers. Use a proprietary flea powder to make sure that none of these unwelcome parasites accompany your birds to the show. You will have taken precautions against scaly leg mite by dunking the legs in surgical spirit about once a month throughout the year, so that should not be a problem. Make sure that claws and beak are trimmed to the correct shape. Dog toenail clippers are the correct shape for this. Check on the correct leg colour for your breed, because if it should be yellow, and the birds have been laying well, the yellow colour will go out of the legs into the yolks. Feeding maize will help to counteract this, as will running the birds on grass. By the same token, if your breed should have white legs, do not feed maize in order to avoid a yellow tinge to the skin.

All shows have an entry date which varies between several weeks before the show to one week before the show. Make sure you enter before this date as late entries are not accepted and check that your entries are correct for the various classes. Show Secretaries will give entry information if asked. Their addresses are in the *Poultry Club Yearbook* under Affiliated Societies, and lists of shows are usually published in the various poultry magazines. If you have shown the previous year, you will normally be sent a schedule. Make sure that your birds are penned in time for judging, and a little oil or vaseline rubbed on the comb, wattles and legs will spruce them up. A silk handkerchief is said to be good for imparting a shine to the feathers, but it is more enduring to have the shine there through good feeding and management in previous months.

Birds are not normally fed or watered in show pens before judging as this can change the correct outline or create dirt and droppings, but take food in the form of grain (firmer droppings) to a show plus water in a container suitable to pour through the bars of a showpen, as not all shows are of sufficient duration to afford stewards to feed and water birds. Water containers are usually provided, but if in doubt, take either a two hook cup drinker or a small plastic container which can be wired, pegged or fixed to the pen so that it does not tip over.

Bear in mind when returning from a show that dusting with flea powder is a sensible precaution, and, ideally, all show birds should be kept separate from your other stock for a few days just to make sure that they have not brought something contagious home from the show, or that the stress of showing has not depressed their immune systems, allowing the entry of disease. A bit of cossetting after a show may well mean that a particular bird can be shown again soon, or return to the breeding pen in a fit condition.

# Appendix 4
# HOUSING AND MANAGEMENT

Poultry housing is used by the birds for roosting, laying and shelter. The welfare of the birds is entirely in your hands and certain principles should therefore be observed.

## Space

The floor area should be a minimum of one square foot per bird (large fowl) or eight square inches for bantams. If you can give them more space then so much the better, bearing in mind they will be spending time in the henhouse sheltering from the rain and wind. Perches should allow a minimum of nine inches for large fowl and six inches for bantams.

## Ventilation

Correct ventilation is vital to prevent the build-up of bacteria and condensation. It should be located near the roof to ensure there are no draughts. It is more difficult keeping the house cool than warm especially in the summer.

## Window

A window is normally located near the roof with a sliding cover to allow for adjusting the ventilation according to the weather and covered in mesh rather than glass due to the danger of breakage. If more than one window is wanted it is best to site them both on the same side so the house can be positioned with its back to the wind. Egg laying is influenced by the amount of light available - the more the merrier.

## Nestboxes

Should be put in the lowest, darkest part of the house as hens like to lay their eggs in secret places. Size for large fowl is up to twelve inches square or eight inches square for bantams with one nestbox per four hens. Communal nestboxes with no partitions are useful as sometimes all the hens choose just one nestbox and queue up or all pile in together, which is when eggs get broken. Make sure there is outside access for you to collect the eggs. Litter in the nestboxes can be shavings or straw, avoiding hay due to mould, and if the nestboxes have a mesh base the fleas find it less welcoming.

## Perches

Even for bantams perches should be broad: two inches square with the top edges rounded is ideal. They should be the correct height for the breed so that they can get onto them easily and have room to stand up on them. See above for spacings, but allow twelve inches between perches if more than one is provided. Make sure they are higher than the nestbox otherwise the hens will roost in the nestbox, fouling it and the eggs. If you can provide a droppings board under the perches which can be removed easily for cleaning this will keep the floor of the house cleaner as hens do two thirds of their droppings at night. You can also check the droppings for colour and consistency more easily.

## Security

The house must provide protection from vermin such as foxes, rats and mice. One inch mesh over ventilation areas will keep out all but the smallest vermin. You may need to be able to padlock the house against two-legged foxes, and do not forget the pophole which, at about a foot square, will be big enough for most birds, with vertical closing safer than sideways closing.

## Materials

Timber should be substantial for the frame and can then be clad with tongue and groove or shiplap or good quality plyboard. If the timber is pressure treated by tanalising or protomising it will last without rotting. The roof needs to be sloping to allow rain to run off, but avoid using felt on the roof as this is where the dreaded red mite likes to breed. Onduline is a corrugated bitumen which is light and warm therefore reducing condensation, or use ply-wood treated with Cuprinol or Timbercare, which is the least toxic wood treatment. To protect the plywood roof further, instead of felt use corrugated plastic as it lets the light through and deters the red mite which likes dark places. Square mesh is best on the window and ventilation areas for strength and sectional construction of the whole unit will make transportation easier.

## Litter

Wood shavings for livestock is the cleanest and best, straw is cheaper, but check that it is fresh and clean, not mouldy or contaminated with vermin or cat excreta. Do not use hay due to the mould spores which will give the hens breathing problems. Litter is used on the floor, in the nestboxes and on the droppings board.

## Floor

The floor can be solid or slatted or mesh. Slats should be 1 ¼ " across with 1" between. If slats are used make sure the house is not off the ground otherwise it will be draughty. Slats or mesh make for easier cleaning out.

## Cleaning

Weekly cleaning is best, replacing litter in all areas. The best disinfectant which is not toxic to the birds is Virkon. This destroys all the bacteria and viruses harmful to the poultry.

## Buy or make?

If housing is bought from a reputable manufacturer and meets all the basic principles, then that may be the quickest and easiest method of housing your birds. If you wish to make housing yourself, keep to the basic principles and remember not to make it too heavy as you will want to move it either regularly or at some stage. Remember also to make the access as easy as possible for you to get in to clean, catch birds or collect eggs. Occasionally second-hand housing becomes available: beware of diseases, rotten timbers and inability to trans-port in sections.

## Types of housing

There are two basic types - movable and static. Movable pens are good as the birds get fresh ground regularly. Some have wheels which makes moving them easy for anyone. Triangular arks were developed to prevent sheep jumping on housing in the days when different stock was ordinarily kept together, but the shape of an ark can damage the comb of a cockerel. The disadvantage of movable pens or fold units is the limit on size and therefore the number of birds kept in each one. Static or free range housing needs to be moved occasionally in order to keep the ground clean around the house, but the hens are allowed to roam freely or contained within a fenced off area. Tall thin houses are unstable in windy areas so go for something low and broad based. If a sliding or hinged roof is incorporated there is no need to have the house high enough for you to stand up in. It is useful to have a free-range house with a solid floor raised off the ground for about eight inches. This discourages rats and other vermin from hiding under the house and can make an extra shelter or dusting area for the birds. They are liable to lay under the house if their nestboxes are inadequate. When using movable pens and moving them on a daily basis it is useful to have feeders and drinkers attached to the unit so it all comes with the unit without having to take the equipment out and put it all back again. If you have a stone or brick building you wish to use as a henhouse, then this is obviously not movable, so you would get round the problem of mud by the door by laying slats or paving slabs or gravel.

When choosing poultry housing go for the basic principles plus ease of access; if a job is easy to do it is more likely to get done, thereby benefitting both you and your birds.


## General management in adverse weather

Frost and snow are the conditions that immediately spring to mind when talking of harsh weather, but what about wind and rain? Poultry are far less able to stand damp and blowy conditions than a good hard frost. When you consider what duvets are traditionally filled with it reinforces the idea that feathers are the finest form of natural insulation known.

The importance of a wind shelter for outdoor birds cannot be overemphasised. The best shape for this, and it does not need a lid, is a cross, so that no matter from which direction the wind blows, the birds can find shelter behind one of the arms. The worst shape is the letter C, as the wind gets trapped in it and creates a massive draught. For draughts are the worst possible conditions for poultry. They just do not thrive, even with top-quality feed, draughts just seem to take the spirit out of them. If your henhouse is not moveable, and therefore not able to be turned with its back to the wind, you can put a windshield in front of the pophole and parallel to it, about three feet away and about four feet high. This will deflect the wind from entering the henhouse with full force. Some people build a tunnel onto their pophole with two right-angled bends in it, which works well if the hens will use it. The secret there is to build it bit by bit so they get used to it gradually. You may consider a henhouse which has to be turned every time the wind changes to be too much like hard work. Practically, the prevailing winds in the UK do not vary that much and the house can be faced east for most of the year, and would only need to be turned about half a dozen times in a year. The hens will sometimes tell you that their house has turned draughty as they will be reluctant to go to bed. Get either yourself or a wet finger in the house at the level of the hens and see what they are complaining about.

Some systems will lend themselves to an eighteen-inch board all around the lower fence in a run, or just where the prevailing wind comes from. The old method of using corrugated tin for the bases of pens did several duties at once, including wind breaks. Keeping foxes out, preventing cocks fighting and lasting for years were the other characteristics of wriggly tin, but the modern stuff is rather thin and doesn't last.

Hens can be immensely stupid in rain. The older ones will quickly decide if it is only a shower or a lasting downpour (you can learn much from watching them and adding a mackintosh accordingly) but young birds are liable to stand around in the wet looking miserable. They will get hypothermia (low body temperature) quite quickly, especially those with thin skulls and crests such as Polands. It is a fast downward spiral as they then do not have the energy to find shelter or food. Do not forget that the wind chill factor increases dramatically if the birds are wet as well.

Most people who suffer (or maybe enjoy) frost and snow regularly during the winter make alternative arrangements for their poultry and house them in airy sheds for the worst months. This lends itself well to giving them extra lighting for early chicks or eggs. Those who live in areas where sometimes you can get away with only the odd night of frost still have to be prepared for those conditions. It is the water that causes the most trouble. Automatic systems have to be abandoned in frosty weather. They are best drained down, as it is somebody's law that they will burst their joints and leak thoroughly if not. The metal galvanized drinkers are a disaster in frosty weather. They seem to freeze quicker than anything else, and if you try and bash the ice out, the galvanising chips and the rust starts. Hot water will of course thaw them, but it is not always convenient to be able to provide hot water. Plastic washing up bowls with tapered sides are an easy and cheap answer to frosty conditions. Only filled half full, when tipped upside down, the ice just slides out, unless you happen to be heavy footed, in which case the bottom of the bowl can join the ice.

Some people put the water in the henhouse at night, assuming the warmth of the hens will keep it from freezing. This may work occasionally, but the old fashioned method of a candle under a clay flowerpot, stood on a flag or bricks is very effective. It is the same principle as the Japanese food-warming trays. The difficulty these days is finding a candle which will last all night. The other alternative is to empty the water at night and fill it in the morning, or take the drinker into your own house for the night.

If the birds are deprived of water for more than the normal night-time abstinence, they get understandably very thirsty. If you then only give them what they normally drink, they will remain thirsty, so if they have been inadvertently deprived, make sure you give them more than the usual amount. Their metabolism will suffer and the production of eggs will stop very quickly if they are short of water. Ideally in really hard weather, fresh water needs to be provided twice a day.

Breeds that have large single combs are prone to frostbite in very severe conditions, which is very painful. Vaseline smeared on the comb will prevent this, or make sure that the henhouse is better insulated than would normally be the case. An extra lining to the roof is sometimes all that is needed. Do not use polystyrene as insulation unless it is covered up as hens adore pecking at it and eating it and it will bung them right up, terminally. If you want to insulate the water bowl , the same applies. A twist of straw around the bowl will keep off a few degrees of frost, or sinking the bowl in a box of polystyrene – well covered up – will also be effective.

Birds that do not often see snow will regard it with horror and not walk on it. You can imagine their consternation when the carpet has changed colour overnight. Put feed and water in the henhouse until they have got used to the new colour, otherwise they are likely to starve themselves. This is where people call them stupid, but their confidence is easily dented, which of course is part of the survival mechanism.

Don't be tempted to give hens extra lighting in harsh weather unless you are prepared to continue with it until the end of March or so (14 hours natural daylight), as their hormone system, which depends on light, will be thoroughly confused with sudden changes in the day length. It can mess up an entire breeding season.

The best feed you can find or afford will definitely help to see your birds through harsh weather. Don't be tempted to change to something you consider better too speedily. If hens do not recognise something as food they will not eat it straight away, and going to bed in the long winter nights with an empty crop is asking for trouble. Feed grain in the evening so that it stays with them longer than pellets would, and introduce any new feed, such as a little maize to help keep them warm, in a gradual way over several days. They really need to be fed, if not ad lib, bearing in mind the attraction to vermin this may cause, at least to capacity, as most of the feed will be going to keeping the hens warm, not leaving much spare for production of eggs or chicks. If you are hatching early, remember to collect eggs several times a day as a frost will ruin embryos, even if it does not actually crack the shell. It is tempting to put early youngsters out in a mild spell in February or March, but this can do more harm than good as it will set them back if the weather turns nasty as they will not know how to deal with it. Heavily sheltered fold units can get round this problem, particularly if the top is rain-proofed. The beginning of March is early enough in most places to get youngsters out, and in the north it will be nearer May.

Experienced poultry keepers will know that cold weather has its benefits in reducing the incidence of disease, but only the canny ones know that walking about with a hen in the winter is a wonderful hand-warmer.

# Appendix 4
# FURTHER READING

**History**

Edward Brown, *Poultry Breeding and Production*, 1929, Caxton (3 vols)

Rev. T.W. Sturges, *The Poultry Manual*, 1921, London

W. B. Tegetmeier, *The Poultry Book*, 1873, London

Harrison Weir, *Our Poultry*, 1902, Hutchinson (2 vols)

Wingfield & Johnson, *The Poultry Book*, 1853, London

Lewis Wright, *Wright's Book of Poultry*, 1919, Waverley

Feathered World Yearbooks, 1912-1938

**Management**

Dr A. Anderson-Brown & G.E.S. Robbins, *The New Incubation Book*, 1992, World Pheasant Association

Dr Clive Carefoot, *Creative Poultry Breeding*, 1988, author

H. Easom Smith, *Managing Poultry for Exhibition*, 1974, Saiga

F.P. Jeffrey, *Bantam Chickens*, 1976, USA

W. Powell-Owen, *The Complete Poultry Book*, 1953, Cassell.

Victoria Roberts, *Diseases of Free Range Poultry*, 1999, Farming Press

Victoria Roberts, *Poultry at Home*, video, 1993, Farming Press

Victoria Roberts (Ed.), *British Poultry Standards*, 1997, Blackwells

Katie Thear, *Free Range Poultry*, 2nd ed. 1997, Farming Press

# GLOSSARY

**Abdomen** underpart of body from keel (breastbone) to vent

**AOC** Any Other Colour

**AOV** Any Other Variety

**Autosexing breeds** breeds developed where the males and females are sexed by colour patterns at day old

**Back** top of body from base of neck to beginning of tail

**Balanced diet** commercial ration necessary for correct growth and bone formation

**Bantam** miniature fowl, one quarter the size of the large version (see also **True Bantam**)

**Barring** alternate stripes of light and dark across a feather, most distinctly seen in the barred Plymouth Rock. Also a genetic factor used in Autosexing breeds

**Bay** a reddish brown colour

**Beak** the two horny mandibles projecting from the front of the face

**Beard** a bunch of feathers under the throat of Faverolles and some colours of Polands

**Beetle brows** heavy overhanging eyebrows seen in Malay and Brahma

**Blade** rear part of a single comb

**Blocky** heavy and square in build

**Booted** feathers projecting from the shanks and toes

**Boule** thick and convexly arched mane in Belgian bantams

**Bow legged** greater distance between legs at hocks than at knees and feet

**Brassiness** yellowish foul colouring on plumage, usually on back and wing

**Breast** front of a fowl's body from point of keel bone to base of the neck

**Breed** a group of birds answering truly to the type, carriage and characteristics distinctive of the breed name they take. Varieties within a breed are distinguished by differences of colour and markings

**Breed Club** an association of fanciers keeping a breed; most clubs organise socials and send out newsletters to their members who pay a small annual subscription

**Broody** the desire of a hen to hatch a clutch of eggs. She will fluff up her feathers and stay in the nestbox. She can be broken off by being secured in a small pen with food and water and out of the elements, with a wire floor for 14 days, or be allowed to sit for the usual 21 days to hatch fowl eggs in a quiet and dark place

**Cape** feathers under and at base of neck hackle, between the shoulders

**Capon** a chemically castrated fowl, now illegal

**Carriage** the bearing, attitude or style of a bird, especially when walking

**Chicks** term applied to poultry from one day old to about 10 weeks when they become 'growers'

**Chicken** term employed to denote a bird of the current season's breeding

**Clean legged** no feathers or feather stubs on the legs

**Cleverness** see **Symmetry**

**Cloddy** heavy and square in build

**Cobby** short, round or compact in build

**Cock** a male bird after the first moult

**Cockerel** a male bird of the current year's breeding

**Comb** fleshy protruberance on top of a fowl's head and varying in shape and size with different breeds

**Commercial diet** or **ration** see **Balanced diet**

**Condition** state of a bird's health, brightness of comb and face and freshness of plumage

**Confined** describing poultry in a fixed area, see also **Fold unit**

**Coverts** covering feathers on tail and wings

**Cow hocks** weakness at hocks, hocks close together instead of well apart

**Crescent** shaped like the first or last quarter of the moon

**Crest** a topknot or tuft of feathers on the head

**Crow head** head and beak narrow and shallow, like a crow

**Cuckoo banding** irregular banding where the two colours (usually grey and dark grey) are somewhat indistinct and run into each other

**Cushion** a mass of feathers over the back of a female covering the root of her tail

**Daw eyed** having pearl coloured eyes like a jackdaw

**Deep litter** method of keeping poultry confined in a stable or shed on the same litter but with more added regularly. If wheat is scattered in the litter then the hens will scratch it over and it will remain friable and dry. See also **Free range, Fold unit** and **Confined**

**Defect** either a deformity in any breed, or a deviation from the Standard for that breed

**Double laced** two lacings of black as on an Indian Game female's body feathers

**Double mating** a system of breeding in a few breeds where the male and female lines are kept separate, one breeding pen producing exhibition males and the other producing exhibition females. Used by some top exhibitors

**Down** initial hairy covering of baby chick

**Drinker** vessel to contain a reservoir of water, so designed that the minimum of muck or litter contaminates it

**Duck footed** fowls having the rear toe lying close to the floor instead of spread out, thus resembling the foot of a duck

**Dusky** yellow pigment shaded with black

**Earlobes** folds of skin hanging below the ears, varying in size, shape and colour

**Ears** the ear canal hidden behind small feathers on the side of the head

**Exhibition** a type of poultry used for showing in competition, some of them having little laying capacity and therefore more often in their "Sunday best" plumage than utility. See Appendix 3

**Face** the skin in front of, behind, and around the eyes

**Feather legged** characteristic of various breeds, may be sparsely feathered down to the outer toes as in Faverolles or profusely feathered to the extremity of middle and outer toes as in Cochins and Brahmas. Serious defect in clean legged breeds

**Feeder** container for feed which avoids contamination by muck or litter and may or may not be used for ad lib feeding

**Fifth toe** an extra toe in some breeds which points upwards forming the letter K with the leg and fourth toe

**Flights** see **Primaries**

**Fluff** soft downy feathers around the thighs of certain breeds

**Fold unit** housing for poultry with a fixed run area, able to be moved on a regular basis over grass usually

**Footings** see **Booted**

**Foxy** rusty or reddish in colour, a defect in some female wings

**Free range** term to describe poultry allowed to wander at will

**Fret marks** structural faults across feathers following some form of stress (weather, poor nutrition)

**Frizzled** curled: each feather turning backwards so that it points towards the head of the bird

**Furnished** feathered and adorned as an adult, used especially for cockerels

**Gay** excess white in markings of plumage

**Ground colour** main colour of body plumage on which markings are applied

**Growers** term used for poultry from 10 weeks until they lay or are mature

**Gullet** resembling a miniature beard of feathers on old Cochin hens

**Gypsy face** the skin of the face a dark purple or mulberry colour

**Hackles** the neck feathers of a fowl and the saddle plumage of a male consisting of long, narrow, pointed feathers

**Handling** method of determining the correct body condition of a bird: Game are firm and corky, the flesh of other breeds is softer, an old or unfit bird is flabby. Used to check for lice especially under the tail

**Hangers** feathers hanging from the posterior part of a male fowl: lesser sickles and tail coverts are known as tail hangers and the saddle hackle as saddle hangers

**Hard Feather** close tight feathering as found on Game birds, a classification

**Hardy** the ability of some breeds to be productive in adverse weather conditions, but see Appendix 4

**Head** comprises skull, comb, face, eyes, beak, earlobes and wattles

**Heavy breeds** a classification of heavier breeds, see Appendix 1

**Hen** a female after the first adult moult

**Hen feathered** a male bird without sickles or pointed hackles as in Sebright

**Hind toe** the fourth or back toe of a fowl

**Hock** joint of the thigh with the shank

**Housing** see Appendix 4

**Hybrid** a cross between breeds

**In kneed** see **Knock kneed**

**Judge** a person who has taken examinations in some or all of the seven sections of poultry, only one exam allowed per year, administered by the **Poultry Club**. There are four Panels: A,B,C,D, A being the highest qualification

**Keel bone** breastbone or sternum

**Knock kneed** hocks close together instead of well apart

**Lacing** a strip or edging all round a feather, differing in colour from that of the ground colour

**Laying trials** in 1930s, breeds in competition, numbers of eggs laid in a certain number of days, plus weight and size of eggs. Done under scientific conditions at various agricultural institutions. Helped with selection for greater egg production

**Leader** the single spike terminating the **Rose comb**

**Leg** the shank or scaly part

**Leg feathers** see **Feather legged**

**Lesser sickles** see **Sickles**

**Light breeds** a classification of breeds generally lighter in weight than the Heavy breeds, see Appendix 1

**Litter** wood shavings or straw as a friable basis in poultry housing

**Lopped comb** single comb falling over to one side of the head, wanted in some females but never in males

**Lustre** see **Sheen**

**Markings** the barring, lacing, pencilling, spangling etc. of the plumage

**Mealy** stippled with a lighter shade, as though dusted with flour

**Moons** round spangles on tips of feathers

**Mossy** confused or indistinct marking, smudging or peppering. A defect in most breeds

**Mottled** marked with tips or spots of different colour

**Muff** tufts of feathers on each side of the face and attached to the beard

**Mulberry** see **Gypsy face**

**Nankin** a yellowish colour named after the cloth, nankeen. Also a rare breed

**Pair** a male and a female

**Pea comb** a triple comb, resembling three small single combs joined together at the base and rear, but distinctly divided, the middle one being the highest

**Pearl eyed** see **Daw eyed**

**Pencilling** small markings or stripes on a feather, straight across in Hamburgh females or concentric in form, following the outline of the feather (Brahma, Cochin, Dorking, Wyandotte)

**Peppering** the effect of sprinkling a darker colour over one of a lighter shade

**Poultry Club** an umbrella organisation for all keepers of poultry, whether utility or exhibition, guardian of the **Standards**. The members get four newsletters per year, a yearbook and the opportunity to partake in the annual National Championship Show (6,000 entries plus) in December

**Primaries** flight feathers of the wing, tucked out of sight when the bird is at rest. Ten in number

**Pullet** a female fowl of the current season's breeding

**Quill** hollow stem of feathers attaching them to the body

**Rare breeds** any breed not having its own **Breed Club**

**Reachy** tall and upright carriage and lift as in Modern Game

**Roach back** hump backed, a deformity

**Rose comb** a broad comb, nearly flat on top, covered with small regular points and finishing with a spike or leader. It varies in length, width and carriage according to breed

**Rust** see **Foxy**

**Saddle** the posterior part of the back, reaching to the tail of the male, and corresponding to the **Cushion** in a female

**Saddle hackle** see **Hackles**

**Secondaries** the quill feathers of the wings which are visible when the wings are closed

**Self colour** a uniform colour of plumage, unmixed with any other

**Serrations** saw-tooth sections of a **Single comb**

**Sexing** possible when birds are about 12 weeks old as hens have rounded feathers on their backs and cocks have pointed feathers on their backs. Comb growth is not necessarily definitive and vent sexing (looking at the genitals) only possible by trained professionals

**Shaft** the stem or quill part of the feather

**Shafty** lighter coloured on the stem than on the webbing, desirable in dark **Dorking** females and Welsummers, generally a defect in other breeds

**Shank** see **Leg**

**Sheen** bright green surface gloss on black plumage. In other colours usually described as **Lustre**

**Shoulder** the upper part of the wing nearest the neck feather

**Sickles** the long curved feathers of a male's tail, usually applied to the top pair only

**Side sprig** an extra spike growing out of the side of a single comb, a defect

**Single comb** a comb which when viewed from the front, is narrow and having spikes in line behind each other. It consists of a blade surmounted by spikes, the lower solid portion being the blade and the spaces between the spikes the serrations. It differs in size, shape and number of serrations according to breed

**Soft Feather** applied to breeds other than the Hard Feather classification, see Appendix 1

**Spangling** the markings produced by a spot of colour at the end of each feather differing from that of the ground colour

**Spike** the rear leader on a **Rose comb**

**Splashed** a contrasting colour irregularly splashed on a feather. In any blue breed when bred they produce blue, black and splashed progeny

**Split crest** divided crest that falls over on both sides

**Split wing** an inherited defect in which the primaries hang below the secondaries when the wing is closed and there is a distinct gap between the primaries and secondaries when the wing is opened

**Spur** a projection of horny substance on the shanks of males, small when young and getting progressively longer with age, and sometimes on females

**Squirrel tail** a tail, any part of which projects in front of a perpendicular line over the back, a tail that bends sharply over the back and touches, or almost touches, the head, like that of a squirrel. A defect in most breeds except Japanese bantams

**Standard** a precise description of all breeds, published in the *British Poultry Standards* (latest edition 1997) and essential for exhibitors and judges. The **Poultry Club** is the guardian of the Standards

**Strain** a family of birds from any breed or variety carefully bred over a number of years

**Striping** very important markings down the middle of hackle feathers, particularly in males of the partridge colours

**Stub** short, partly grown feather

**Symmetry** perfection of outline, proportion, harmony of all parts. Known as **Cleverness** in Game

**Tail feathers** straight and stiff feathers of the tail only. The top pair are sometimes slightly curved, but they are generally straight. In the male fowl, main tail feathers are contained inside the sickles and coverts

**Tassel** a form of crest in Game

**Thigh** the leg above the shank and covered in feathers

**Ticked** plumage tipped with a different colour, usually applied to V-shaped markings as in Ancona

**Tipping** end of feathers tipped with a different coloured marking

**Treading** the act of mating

**Trio** a male and two females

**True bantam** one of nine breeds which do not have a large version, see Appendix 1

**Type** mould or shape, see **Symmetry**

**Undercolour** colour seen when a bird is handled, that is when the feathers are lifted: colour of fluff of feathers

**Uropygium** Parson's nose, lack of which makes a rumpless breed

**Utility** generally any breed of poultry which earns its keep by laying, producing meat or being broody. Not usually exhibited as they tend to be always in 'working clothes'. See Appendix 2

**Variety** a definite branch of a breed known by its distinctive colour or markings

**Vent** orifice from where either an egg is laid or faeces are produced, the two processes being entirely separate

**Vulture hocks** stiff projecting quill feathers at the hock joint growing on the thighs and extending backwards

**Wattles** the fleshy appendages at each side of the base of the beak, more strongly developed in male birds

**Web** a flat or thin structure as in web of feather

**Wing bar** any line of dark colour across the middle of the wing

**Wing bay** the triangular part of the folded wing between the wing bar and the point

**Wing bow** the upper or shoulder part of the wing

**Wing coverts** the feathers covering the roots of the secondaries

**Work** the small spikes or working on top of a rose comb

**Wry tail** a tail carried awry, to the right or the left side, a defect

# INDEX